The Origins of Ethical Failures

In 2001, as a young university graduate, Dennis Gentilin became a member of a FX trading desk at one of Australia's largest banks, the National Australia Bank. In the years that followed the desk became involved in a trading scandal that resulted in the resignation of the chairman and CEO, the upheaval of the board of directors, significant financial loss, and incalculable reputational damage. It was in this environment that the true meaning of business ethics was revealed to Gentilin.

In this ground breaking book, Gentilin draws on both his personal experience and the emerging literature in the various disciplines of psychology to provide a very unique insight into the origins of ethical failures. The intellectual depth Gentilin provides coupled with his real life reflections make this book a must read for senior leaders, regulators, consultants, academics and practitioners.

Amongst other things, the book highlights the shortcomings associated with the traditional approaches used to explain and address ethical failures and illustrates how easily we can all, individuals and organisations alike, be complicit to unethical conduct. More importantly, it provides lessons and guidance to all leaders who aspire to build institutions that are more resilient to ethical failure.

In his 15 years in financial services, Dennis Gentilin has been an advocate for ethical practice in the industry. His time in financial markets was defined by his very client centered and values based approach to his work. More recently, he has been central to the development and deployment of a framework that has transformed how performance is measured and rewarded for the top 200 leaders at the National Australia Bank. Gentilin has written the occasional article for *The Ethics Centre* and the *Banking Finance Oath* (BFO). His most recent contribution was titled 'The BFO is the first step in a long journey'. He has also appeared as a guest lecturer at the Executive MBA programme at his alma mater Monash University, located in Melbourne, Australia.

To Troff, who showed me "the way"

The Origins of Ethical Failures

Lessons for Leaders

DENNIS GENTILIN

Routledge
Taylor & Francis Group

LONDON AND NEW YORK

First published 2016
by Routledge
2 Park Square, Milton Park, Abingdon, Oxon OX14 4RN

and by Routledge
711 Third Avenue, New York, NY 10017

Routledge is an imprint of the Taylor & Francis Group, an informa business

British Library Cataloguing-in-Publication Data
A catalogue record for this book is available from the British Library

Library of Congress Cataloging-in-Publication Data
The Library of Congress Data has been applied for

ISBN: 978-1-4724-7761-3 (hbk)
ISBN: 978-1-138-69051-6 (pbk)
ISBN: 978-1-4724-7762-0 (ebk – ePDF)
ISBN: 978-1-4724-7763-7 (ebk – ePUB)

Typeset in Palatino Linotype
by Apex CoVantage, LLC

Contents

List of Figures   *vii*
List of Tables   *ix*
About the Author   *xi*
Acknowledgements   *xiii*
Foreword   *xv*

Introduction   **1**

1   The Power of Context   **7**
Social Norms   8
Stanford Prison Experiment   21
The Role of Leadership   25
Lessons for Leaders   36
Where to Next?   38

2   Group Dynamics   **45**
Power and Obedience   47
The (Innocent?) Bystander   54
Majority Influence   56
Group Polarisation   60
Ethical Followership   63
Lessons for Leaders   70
Where to Next?   73

3   Our Flawed Humanity   **79**
Are Humans Self-Interested?   80
Money   87
Power   102
Fear   109
Lessons for Leaders   115
Where to Next?   119

4   What We Fail to See   **127**
The Slippery Slope   128

Loss Aversion and Framing   132
Overconfidence   138
Moral Disengagement   141
Lessons for Leaders   144

Conclusion   **157**
Education   158
Chief Ethics Officer   161
Lessons for Leaders   163

Index   *167*

List of Figures

Figure I.1   The antecedents of ethical failures   5

Figure 1.1   Percentage of participants who littered after entering a
               car park that was either heavily littered (descriptive "pro-
               littering" norm) or had all the litter neatly swept into piles
               (injunctive "no littering" norm). These norms were made
               salient by having an accomplice of the experimenters litter
               in full view of the participants causing their attention to be
               drawn to the condition of the car park   11
Figure 1.2   Percentage of participants sending a truthful message to
               their partner after learning how a person facing the same
               dilemma would respond   12
Figure 1.3   Performance of participants in an arithmetic task in the
               following four scenarios: (a) normal test conditions
               (baseline), (b) participants provided with the opportunity
               to cheat, (c) cheating modeled by a peer considered to be a
               member of the "in-group", and (d) cheating modeled by a
               peer considered to be a member of an "out-group"   15
Figure 1.4   Median light movement (in inches) established in each
               scenario across 11 trials. The final eight trials are those where
               there were no accomplices of the experimenters
               planted in any of the groups   17
Figure 1.5   Average number of imitative aggressive responses
               reproduced by children after viewing an adult role model
               behaving aggressively towards a Bobo doll. The adult
               role model was either punished, rewarded or faced no
               consequences for their aggressive behaviour. Some of the
               children were offered rewards to reproduce the aggressive
               behaviour while others were offered no reward   30

Figure 2.1   Percentage of participants obeying the instructions of
               the experimenter at each shock level of the Milgram
               obedience studies   51
Figure 2.2   An example of the two cards that were shown to
               participants in the experiments conducted by Solomon
               Asch   57

Figure 2.3   Percentage of children trick-or-treating in groups or alone
                who disobeyed the experimenter. Some children were
                required to identify themselves by providing personal details
                (non-anonymous) while others remained anonymous   63

Figure 3.1   The payoffs associated with the Prisoner's Dilemma Game   83
Figure 3.2   Participants in the wealthy group completed the anagram
                task in a room that contained a table with approximately
                $7,000 cash on it   93
Figure 3.3   The percentage of participants who actually and claimed to
                have created 12 words in the anagram task. The wealthy
                group completed the anagram task in a room containing a
                table with approximately $7,000 cash on it, while the room
                in which the poor group completed the task in contained a
                table with sufficient cash on it to cover the maximum reward
                the participants could potentially earn from their involvement
                in the study   94
Figure 3.4   Amount of money in the jars (displayed as averages).
                For each of the three scenarios, the results display the
                following outcomes: (a) the actual amount of money in the
                jar, (b) the amount the advisor predicted was in the jar, (c) the
                amount the advisor suggested to the estimator was in the jar,
                and (d) the amount the estimator predicted was in the jar
                after learning of the advisor's suggestion   97

Figure 4.1   National Australia Bank currency options portfolio Value
                at Risk, January 2003 to January 2004   132
Figure 4.2   Percentage of cooperative responses in the first round and
                across all seven trials of the "Community Game" and the
                "Wall Street Game". Participants played the game in pairs,
                where both members of the pair were selected on the basis
                that they were more likely to "cooperate" or more likely
                to "defect"   136
Figure 4.3   Performance in the "matrix task" in one of three scenarios: (a)
                normal test conditions, (b) opportunity for cheating, and (c)
                opportunity for cheating and requirement to sign honour
                code. In each scenario, some students were awarded $0.50
                for each correctly solved matrix, while others were
                awarded $2.00   146

List of Tables

Table 1.1   The matrices used in the study conducted by Gino and her
            colleagues contained 12 numbers written to two decimal places.
            Participants in the study were required to find the two numbers
            in the matrix that summed to ten   14

Table 4.1   The estimates of the amount of money in the jar that
            participants were required to accept or reject. As can be
            seen, for rounds 11 to 16 inclusive, the estimates provided
            were identical   130

Table 4.2   Amount of overstatement in the value of the currency options
            portfolio at the National Australia Bank   131

About the Author

Dennis Gentilin is a financial services professional who has been employed in the banking industry for over 15 years. His first ten years were spent working in a variety of roles in financial markets, and more recently he worked within corporate strategy.

Without question Dennis's defining career moment was his association with the FX trading scandal that rocked the National Australia Bank (NAB) in 2004. Although he was publicly named as a "whistleblower" in that incident, he has been reluctant to allow this label to define him (for better or worse) and become central to his identity.

This being said, it goes without saying that this experience profoundly shaped Dennis and his view of the world. What's more, his inquisitive nature and capacity for deep thought means that he reflected on the incident like very few would, allowing him to develop a unique perspective on business ethics.

It is only recently that Dennis felt compelled to share his insights. The result is this very unique business book that combines a memoir on a real life experience with a meditation on our flawed humanity. Within these pages Dennis has managed to salvage, in a way very few could, the lessons associated with an ethical failure.

Dennis's primary motivation for writing *The Origins of Ethical Failures* is to educate. He hopes that the lessons herein will be valuable to all leaders, and illustrate the central role they play in creating institutions that are more resilient to unethical conduct.

However, in addition, Dennis hopes the book will play a role in continuing the push we have seen in recent times that looks to make ethics a key priority in the business world. As he himself says, the costs associated with failing to do this are too great:

> *Ethical failures produce no winners. The victims are not just those found guilty of engaging in illegal or unethical conduct. Community*

and customers lose faith in a brand they once believed in, shareholders suffer considerable losses, and employees are left to deal with the drawn out consequences associated with loss of trust and greater scrutiny. Ultimately, society at large carries the cost.

Dennis lives in Melbourne, Australia with his wife Kate and two daughters Amelia and Charlotte.

Acknowledgements

To my colleagues at NAB, past and present, whose support and encouragement has meant a great deal to me. To Vanessa Kirby – who would have thought a neighbour would make such a great research assistant? To my local editor Ann Bolch for her early guidance. To Mary Gentile, who made me believe I had produced something of value that deserved to sit on a bookshelf. To Lindsay Tanner, whose wisdom and counsel took this project down a very different path. To Michaela Healey, who never flinched and was "bold". To the NAB, who at no stage requested any edits to be made to the content of this book and were at all times incredibly supportive – the messaging and symbolism associated with this stance cannot be underestimated. To my wife Kate, who each time I come up with a crazy idea like returning to university to study psychology, riding from Sydney to Hobart to raise money for cancer, or writing a book, just rolls her eyes and then gets right behind me.

Foreword

In January 2004 a "whistleblower" in the currency options team at the National Australia Bank (NAB) raised concerns about the team's trading position. Two weeks of internal investigation revealed $360 million in losses due to unauthorised transactions. By mid-February 2004 both the bank's CEO and chairman had resigned. Four currency traders and their supervisor were dismissed and the bank's executive general managers of corporate and institutional banking, markets and risk were replaced. One of the traders, head of the foreign currency options desk, subsequently received a gaol sentence. Of course, the biggest losers, collectively, were NAB shareholders. As investors lost confidence in a corporate culture that could incubate this sort of employee behaviour, NAB's share price plunged and the organisation quickly lost its status as Australia's biggest bank. Ultimately, the losses suffered by shareholders were several multiples of the financial losses incurred by the currency options team.

Whistleblowing takes a great deal of courage. And it is easy to understand why those who do blow the whistle on their colleagues might want to walk away from an organisation that had put them in such a difficult position. Instead of walking away, Dennis Gentilin asked himself "why?". The behaviours that he had observed, and which had led him to blow the whistle, were not obvious instances of people confronting an ethical dilemma, having to choose between "right" and "right"; rather, people were choosing "wrong". Was this because of who they were (a few "bad apples") or because of the situation in which they found themselves (a "rotten barrel")?

This book was motivated by a particular set of experiences in a particular corporation. But this is not a book principally about those experiences, nor is it a book principally about the NAB. This is a book about business ethics with general applicability. The questions it raises are those that affect all businesses. And the lessons will prove valuable to those with leadership (and "followership") responsibilities in all commercial organisations; to all of those who have a responsibility to insist on compliance with rules, regulations and other artefacts of governance, but who know that their most important obligation is to lead, through character and morality, the development of an ethical business culture.

Successful leaders will embrace humility. All organisations are fallible. And the coercive imposition of rules and regulations, and even credible transparency mechanisms, cannot be relied upon to ensure ethical conduct; in certain cases these can even make things worse.

There are no simple answers in this book. But there are answers. And there are important truths, supported by deep and rigorous analysis. These should be of interest to all corporate leaders, in both executive and non-executive roles. One such truth is that "leaders must strive to articulate a meaningful social purpose for their organisations that is underpinned by a virtuous set of values". Not all corporate leaders will appreciate the connection between this proposition and the enhancement of shareholder value; that is, until they read this book.

Dr Ken R. Henry AC, NAB Chairman

Introduction

If only there were evil people somewhere insidiously committing evil deeds, and it were necessary only to separate them from the rest of us and destroy them. But the line dividing good and evil cuts through the heart of every human being.[1]

Aleksandr Solzhenitsyn, The Gulag Archipelago

WHY CAN'T THE BANKING INDUSTRY SOLVE ITS ETHICS PROBLEMS?

Neil Irwin, *The New York Times*, 29 July 2014.

The financial crisis that nearly brought down the global economy was triggered in no small part by the aggressive culture and spotty ethics within the world's biggest banks. But after six years and countless efforts to reform finance, the banking scandals never seem to end.

The important question that doesn't yet have a satisfying answer is why.

Why are the ethical breaches at megabanks so routine that it is hard to keep them straight? Why do banks seem to have so many scandals—and ensuing multimillion dollar legal settlements—compared with other large companies like retailers, airlines or manufacturers?

Some of the world's leading bank regulators are trying to figure that out. And they have taken to sounding like parents who have grown increasingly exasperated at teenage children who keep wrecking the family car.

After reading the beginning of this article by Neil Irwin, my first response was to check the date it was published. Had I accidently clicked on a link that took me to an article written five or maybe ten years earlier? Is Neil Irwin caught is some sort of time warp? Surely, with everything that we have experienced and learned, we are still not angered, discouraged and perplexed by the poor behaviour of bankers?

Sadly, I was mistaken. Although I had been toying with the idea of writing a book on the origins of ethical failures in business for some time, reading this article made me realise I had no choice but to insert myself into the conversation. Not that the conversation needed another person expressing a view, but I believed I had a contribution to make. And for good reason.

My first foray into corporate life exposed me to an experience that brought to life the issue of ethics as it applies to the business world in the most dramatic of ways. As a young, bright-eyed and impressionable graduate, I joined a team that became involved in a FX trading scandal that resulted in the resignation of the chairman and CEO, the upheaval of the board of directors, significant financial loss and incalculable reputational damage to one of Australia's largest banks, the National Australia Bank (NAB). In the years that followed the incident and subsequent court cases, there was one question that preoccupied me and continues to fascinate me today. How could a group of intelligent, well-educated people from privileged backgrounds be involved in behaviour which was by anyone's measure clearly unethical?

What made this question even more intriguing was the nature of the ethical dilemmas that were faced by both the traders and the leaders within the business, that are typical of the majority of the dilemmas underpinning the well-known ethical failures that have plagued the banking and finance industry and the broader business world. The ethical dilemmas did not involve a decision between "right versus right", where one must make an excruciating choice between competing moral values.[2] Rather, they involved "right versus wrong" decisions, where a choice needed to be made between an alternative that was clearly ethical and one that was clearly not. That is to say, the dilemmas pitted a moral value against basic self-interest, and in the end self-interest won out, despite what was ethical and "right" being clearly distinguishable from what was unethical and "wrong".

At the time of the FX trading scandal, the field of business ethics primarily focused on compliance. This is hardly surprising as scholars in the field adopted the so-called "normative" approach, which assumes that individuals are rational, self-interested beings who are aware of the ethical dilemmas they face and understand the implications of unethical conduct (so-called *homo economicus*). This approach is compelling because it is both simple and intuitive – people understand the rules, and if they break them they do so knowingly, fully understanding the implications. My experience illustrated to me in no uncertain terms the shortcomings of this approach. What's more, the litany of ethical scandals that have occurred since the FX trading incident, despite the heightened focus on compliance, further illustrate that rules, regulation and governance are only part of the story.

This does not mean that compliance has no role to play in promoting ethical conduct. To the contrary. Boundaries are required, but once established, boundaries can and will be broken. As Oscar Wilde famously said, "I can resist everything but temptation" – compliance and regulation cannot engender character and morality. I have spent the years since the trading scandal searching for an explanation as to why people don't behave as the normative approach dictates. Why do intelligent, well educated individuals transgress ethical boundaries when confronted by them? And what's more, why do these same individuals transgress these boundaries even though doing so is clearly unethical?

Serendipitously, when I joined the trading desk as a graduate, the field of behavioural business ethics began to emerge. Behavioural business ethics is the point of intersection between the fields of business ethics and psychology, and attempts to address the shortcomings of the normative approach. Namely, the field attempts to provide explanations for why humans, when faced with an ethical dilemma, respond in ways that the normative approach would label irrational. Behavioural business ethics has provided significant insight into the topic of business ethics, and more importantly, many of its key findings speak to my experience. By highlighting these key findings, this book builds a coherent narrative to explain the why: Why unethical conduct is and will continue to be part of the business world.

There is a cautionary note for readers here. Although insightful, we must be careful on how we interpret and apply the findings emanating from the research in this field. Specifically, making conclusions about its broader applicability must be done prudently. Like research from any domain, there is always a question mark over whether the findings can be applied to real-life settings (the so-called "external validity"). This is especially the case when the research is conducted in a laboratory, where the context and participants (in the case of psychology typically undergraduate university students) are not representative of that which exists in the setting to which the findings are being applied. Readers who follow the field of psychology would be familiar with the reproducibility project – the results from its recent attempt to replicate the findings of 100 psychological studies were sobering and illustrative of this point.[3] They provide cause for pause and reflection among both psychologists and those who report on and apply their findings. This cautionary note aside, it would also be remiss to neglect or underestimate the insight provided by the field. The sheer volume of the findings, coupled with the calibre of the academics behind it, make it very compelling.

In addition to borrowing from the field of behavioural business ethics, this book also draws heavily from my own personal experience on the trading desk. This is not done to explain the what, when, who and how of the incident – this has been adequately covered in other publications.[4] Rather, the insights this experience has provided me with are used to complement the theory. Readers should not assume that the key lessons from the book are therefore only relevant to the world of financial markets. My subsequent corporate experience and research into other cases of unethical conduct have taught me that there are similar dynamics underpinning most of the well-documented ethical failures. Be it phone hacking in journalism, drug taking in cycling or rate fixing in financial markets, there are parallels in how the unethical conduct associated with these events originated. Where possible the book draws on examples from other ethical failures to illustrate this point.

I have not written this book as an academic, a philosopher or an ethicist. Rather, I have written this book as a practitioner, in the truest sense of the word. My objectives are fourfold. Firstly, I aim to enlighten leaders in the business world of how unethical behaviour can occur, despite the presence of robust governance and compliance frameworks. Secondly, I want to illustrate how explanations for unethical behaviour are not straightforward – reasons for unethical conduct are multi-layered and complex. Thirdly, I hope to make leaders recognise that we are all susceptible to unethical conduct, regardless of how scrupulous our characters may be. Finally, I want to illustrate the central role leaders play in developing cultures that are more resistant to ethical failures, and cultures that are better equipped to deal with the fall out of unethical behaviour when it occurs.

Leaders need to be warned that building ethical cultures is not easy. There is no technical solution to this challenge, no lever that can be pulled to drive ethical conduct among all of an organisation's employees. Creating an ethical culture is a classic adaptive problem, because it involves winning the hearts and minds of employees. As Ronald Heifetz and Marty Linsky outline in their book *Leadership on the Line*, adaptive problems require a special type of leadership, because by challenging people's "habits, beliefs and values", they stimulate resistance.[5] They go onto say:

> *Because real leadership – the kind that surfaces conflict, challenges long-held beliefs, and demands new ways of doing things – causes pain. And when people feel threatened, they take aim at the person pushing for change.*

The ultimate objective when building an ethical culture is to institutionalise an organisation's code of ethics, so that each employee lives and breathes the document. Compliance and regulation alone cannot create such a culture. As this book will illustrate, through their actions, choices and decisions, leaders play a central role in ensuring that the standards established by the code are brought to life within their organisations. This requires significant effort, but the rewards make the investment worthwhile.

Given the work required to build ethical cultures is adaptive in nature, this book does not attempt to develop new theories or frameworks – doing so would be creating a technical fix for an adaptive problem. Rather, the book draws on the research in psychology and my own personal experiences to highlight the origins of unethical behaviour in the business world. The first chapter explores the contextual, and how the system in which one operates, despite often being overlooked, is arguably the most significant driver of unethical behaviour as it can shape our moral character. Chapter two looks at the relational, and highlights how dysfunctional group dynamics can cause people to condone behaviours and decisions they would ordinarily consider to be totally inappropriate when acting alone. Chapter three explores the personal, focusing on three factors that exist in all organisations that can bring out the worst in our flawed humanity,

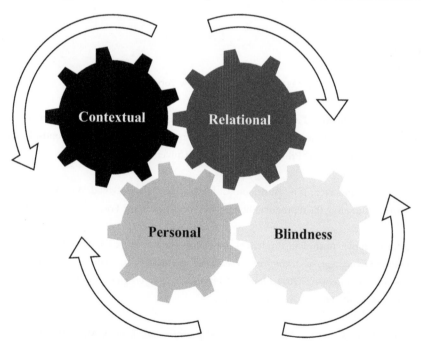

Figure I.1   The antecedents of ethical failures

namely money, power and fear. Finally, chapter four shows how faults in our cognitions can lead to blindness, causing us to behave unethically without realising we are doing so. As Figure I.1 illustrates, although they are presented separately, these concepts are not mutually exclusive. Rather they overlap and work together to drive ethical failures. The conclusion explores the role of education and the chief ethics officer, and summarises the lessons for leaders that appear throughout the book.

The world is yearning for leaders with an ethical dimension, leaders who not only demonstrate through their actions, choices and decisions a grounding in sound ethical principles, but who also understand that their obligations stretch far beyond themselves and the organisation and stakeholders they serve. These are the leaders who can begin restoring some faith in the institutions that play such a significant role in our economy. Just as there is no panacea for the creation of ethical cultures, there is also no panacea for the creation of ethical leaders – as humans we are all susceptible to ethical shortcomings. Ethical leadership requires thinking, practice, reflection and a lot of hard work. For those of us who are prepared to undertake the hard work involved, an understanding of the circumstances that can lead to unethical conduct is vital as we embark on the journey.

Notes

[1]   Solzhenitsyn, A. I. (1973). *The Gulag Archipelago*. New York, NY: Harper & Row.

[2]   These types of dilemmas are classically illustrated by the so-called "trolley problem" which is comprehensively reviewed by David Edmonds in the following book: Edmonds, D. (2014). *Would you kill the fat man?* Princeton, NJ: Princeton University Press.

[3]   Aarts, A. A., Anderson, J. E., Anderson, C. J., Attridge, P. R., Attwood, A., Axt, J., . . . Zuni, K. (2015). Estimating the reproducibility of psychological science. *Science, 349*(6251), aac4716.

[4]   See for example: Australian Prudential Regulatory Authority. (2004, March 23). *Report into irregular currency options trading at the National Australia Bank*. Sydney, Australia: Author; PricewaterhouseCoopers. (2004, March 12). *Investigation into foreign exchange losses at the National Australia Bank*. Melbourne, Australia: Author.

[5]   Heifetz, R. A., & Linsky, M. (2002). *Leadership on the line*. Boston, MA: Harvard Business School Publishing.

I

The Power of Context

Contextual

The search for scapegoats is essentially an abnegation of responsibility: It indicates an inability to assess honestly and intelligently the true nature of the problems which lie at the root of social and economic difficulties and a lack of resolve in grappling with them.[1]

Aung San Suu Kyi, Freedom
from Fear

As humans, we are all compromised to some degree. Although free will dictates that we are in control of the decisions and choices we make, we fail to recognise how the environment within which we find ourselves plays a significant role in shaping our decisions and choices, sometimes in far more subtle ways than we appreciate. Similarly, in the business world, the environment within which one operates is a primary driver of behaviour, ethical or otherwise. Developed by Gerald Salancik and Jeffrey Pfeffer in the 1970s, social information process theory supports this notion that in the workplace, employees will look for cues in the environment for guidance on how to behave, especially when facing an ambiguous or uncertain situation.[2]

Despite this, explanations of unethical conduct rarely give proper consideration to the system within which people operate. A major reason for this is that as humans we have a propensity to simplify the complex (a topic we visit in chapter four), and one way we do this is by looking for associations and inferring causality. Therefore, explanations of unethical behaviour tend to focus on identifying "bad apples" or "rogues", and assigning responsibility to these individuals. This approach instantly provides a cause for unethical conduct, and provides a simple and intuitive explanation.

As this book will illustrate, explaining unethical behaviour is complex and rarely that straightforward and simple. As a starting point, any explanation of unethical behaviour must consider the environment within which the "bad apples" operate, recognising that it can have a profound effect on behviour. What's more, if an assessment of the environment reveals a rotten "barrel", then one will also find that the unethical behaviour is rarely constrained to a few "bad apples" – it has more than likely permeated the system. Therefore, when exploring the origins of unethical behaviour, the "barrel" within which the "bad apples" operate must be given as much (if not more) attention as the "bad apples" themselves.

One of the best-known studies in social psychology that illustrates how the environment can have a profound impact on human behaviour is the Stanford Prison Experiment. Conducted in 1971, the study vividly highlights how situational forces can drive ordinary people to behave in ways which are not only totally out of character, but also contrary to what most people would consider to be appropriate and ethical. Before discussing this experiment and some of the key lessons it provides, a concept from social psychology will be introduced that is highly relevant to understanding "situational determinism" and how context shapes our behaviours – social norms.

Social Norms

> Kaffee: Corporal, would you turn to the page in this book that says
>   where the enlisted men's mess hall is?
> Howard: Lt. Kaffee, that's not in the book, sir.
> Kaffee: I don't understand, how did you know where the enlisted
>   men's mess hall was if it's not in this book?
> Howard: I guess I just followed the crowd at chow time, sir.[3]
>
> A Few Good Men

Robert Cialdini and Melanie Trost developed the following definition of social norms:[4]

> Social norms are rules and standards that are understood by members
> of a group, and that guide and/or constrain social behaviour without the
> force of laws. These norms emerge out of interaction with others; they
> may or may not be stated explicitly, and any sanctions for deviating
> from them come from social networks, not the legal system.

Social norms play a very important role in governing group behaviour and structure, as they organise social interactions (e.g. "do not interrupt others"), provide direction and motivation (e.g. "don't arrive late to a meeting"), make other people's responses predictable and meaningful (e.g. "acknowledge someone when they greet you") and generally identify what is normal practice and what is not. There are two properties of social norms that differentiate them from rules or regulations. Firstly, they are emergent, in that they develop gradually over time as group members interact and their behaviours align. Secondly, they are consensual, as they are standards of behaviour that are ostensibly endorsed by members of the group. In short, despite not being visible, social norms can profoundly influence human behaviour.

Psychologists make a distinction between *injunctive* and *descriptive* norms. Injunctive norms prescribe the behaviour that is socially valued and specify what constitutes morally approved and disapproved conduct. Descriptive norms meanwhile refer to how people actually behave, and tend to be relied upon in novel, ambiguous or uncertain situations. Therefore, where injunctive norms specify what *ought* to be done, descriptive norms specify what *is* done.

There has been an extraordinary amount of research conducted into how social norms emerge and drive human behaviour, much of which is relevant to the realm of business ethics. Three patterns that have emerged in this research that are of particular relevance are described below.

I. UNETHICAL DESCRIPTIVE NORMS CAN OVERRIDE INJUNCTIVE NORMS

Although research continues to explore what causes people to adopt descriptive or injunctive norms,[5] saliency is recognised as being a major contributing factor. As we will see, when our attention is drawn to a descriptive norm, there is a strong likelihood it will dictate how we behave, even if the behaviour it prescribes is unethical. It is this pattern that is at the heart of many of the well-documented ethical failures that involve a conflict between doing what is morally "right" and what is clearly unethical and "wrong". In these situations, the descriptive norms dominate and override the injunctive norms, and what *is* done is at odds with what *ought* to be done.

In one of the classic studies investigating how injunctive and descriptive norms operate, Robert Cialdini and his colleagues explored the social norms surrounding littering.[6] Imagine you are a participant in the study. You are leaving a hospital and upon entering the car park you witness an individual, who unbeknown to you happens to be an accomplice of the experimenters, litter the car park with a pamphlet. This draws your attention to the condition of the car park. For some participants the car park was heavily littered, while for other participants the litter was neatly swept into three piles. Upon returning to your vehicle, you find a pamphlet beneath the driver's side windscreen wiper. Do you dispose of the pamphlet on the floor of the car park?

Cialdini and his colleagues designed the experiment so that the heavily littered car park pointed to a descriptive norm promoting littering, while the neatly swept car park pointed to the no littering injunctive norm. The purpose of having an accomplice litter in full view of the participants was to draw their attention to these norms and make them more salient. In some trials, the accomplice of the experimenters simply walked by the participant without littering so that a basis for comparison could be established. As illustrated in Figure 1.1, the results show an interesting pattern. In a highly littered car park, a participant was far more likely to litter when their attention was drawn to the pro-littering descriptive norm suggested by the condition of the car park. However, when participants entered a car park where the litter was neatly swept into piles, this pattern was reversed. Participants littered less when their attention was drawn to the no littering injunctive norm.

Now many of us may question whether littering a hospital car park qualifies as unethical behaviour (I'll let others be the judge of this). Surely in situations with greater ethical consequence people would see through the descriptive norm and behave in a way that is aligned to the injunctive norm? Consider a study conducted by Brian Gunia and his colleagues, where participants were informed that they were working on a "decision-making task" with an anonymous individual while sitting at a computer terminal.[7] The task required that $15 be split between the participant and their anonymous partner in one of two ways. Option A would provide the participant with $10 and the partner with $5, while option B would provide the participant with $5 and the partner with $10. Only the participant was aware of these monetary payoffs.

The participant's partner was required to select between options A or B, and to aid them in making the decision, the participant sent them one of two messages. One was a truthful message ("option B earns you more than option A") and the other was a lie ("option A earns you more than option B"). Upon being presented with this dilemma, the participants were told that they were able to exchange messages with another randomly selected participant facing

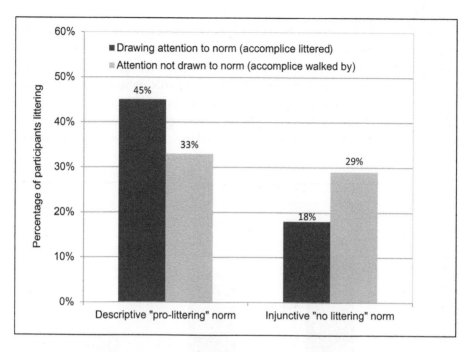

Figure 1.1   Percentage of participants who littered after entering a car park that was either heavily littered (descriptive "pro-littering" norm) or had all the litter neatly swept into piles (injunctive "no littering" norm). These norms were made salient by having an accomplice of the experimenters litter in full view of the participants causing their attention to be drawn to the condition of the car park

Source: Cialdini, R. B., Reno, R. R., & Kallgren, C. A. (1990). A focus theory of normative conduct: Recycling the concept of norms to reduce littering in public places. *Journal of Personality and Social Psychology, 58*(6), 1015–1026.

the same predicament. The randomly chosen participant was non-existent but sent the participants one of the following three messages:

- *Moral message*: I am planning to send the truthful message as most people would be honest in these situations.

- *Immoral message*: I am planning to send the message that maximises my payoffs as most people would see the pursuit of self-interest as appropriate in these situations.

- *Neutral message*: I am undecided as to how I will respond as most people would have a hard time deciding how to behave in these situations.

As Figure 1.2 illustrates, when the "conversation partner" highlighted the moral choice, the majority of the participants (80 per cent) sent the truthful message. However, when the participant's attention was drawn to the immoral, self-interested alternative, only half of participants chose to send the truthful message. Therefore, even when facing situations with heavier moral weight, if what *is* done is not aligned with what *ought* to be done, people can be swayed to select an immoral course of action if they see similar others adopting this approach.

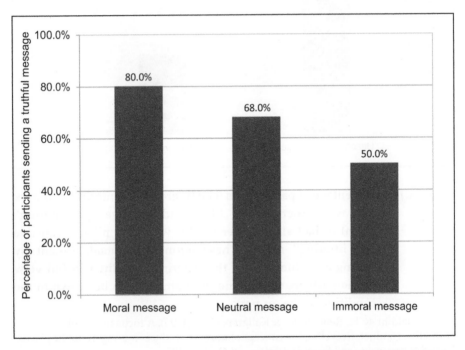

Figure 1.2   **Percentage of participants sending a truthful message to their partner after learning how a person facing the same dilemma would respond**

Source: Gunia, B. C., Wang, L., Huan, L., Wang, J., & Murnighan, J. K. (2012). Contemplation and conversation: Subtle influences on moral decision making. *Academy of Management Journal, 55*(1), 13–33.

From a business ethics perspective, there are two insights that can be taken from these studies. Firstly, environmental cues, no matter how subtle, can cause us to behave in inappropriate and unethical ways. In neither of these scenarios were participants working under instructions or following the orders provided by an authoritative leader. They were simply guided by observing what was occurring around them.

Secondly, and perhaps more importantly, we often see organisations engage in initiatives that attempt to draw employees' attention to the injunctive norm for ethical behaviour. For example, they may develop codes prescribing ethical behaviour, have their employees swear allegiance to these codes, require compulsory attendance at training programmes promoting compliance, or have top management issue finely crafted communication encouraging moral conduct. If the behaviour of people within organisations neglects or is at odds with what these initiatives prescribe, then they will more than likely fail in their intention to drive ethical behaviour. As we will see later in the chapter, this is especially the case when the people in positions of power within organisations are those displaying the inconsistent behaviour.

2. GROUP IDENTIFICATION AND SOCIAL NORMS

In a paper published in 1979, Henri Tajfel and John Turner provided a theory of intergroup behaviour known as social identity theory.[8] A core premise of their theory is that group membership, be it at the micro level (for e.g. a group within a workplace or a local sporting team) or the macro level (for e.g. a country or race), provides members with a social identity which prescribes how one should think and behave. Thus, the groups we belong to play a central role in providing us with a point of reference in helping us determine whether our actions are appropriate and morally acceptable.

In a range of experiments leading up to the formulation of social identity theory, it was shown consistently that categorising participants randomly into two separate groups generated in-group favouritism and discrimination against the out-group.[9] This in-group bias means that questionable behaviour may in many instances be condoned and accepted as an appropriate social norm if it is performed by someone belonging to our in-group, or alternatively be scorned upon and labelled as unethical if performed by a member of the out-group.

Francesca Gino and her colleagues conducted a clever experiment illustrating this pattern of behaviour.[10] In it, undergraduate university students participated in a five-minute assessment requiring them to complete a relatively straightforward arithmetic task.[11] The participants were provided with a worksheet containing 20 matrices. Each matrix contained 12 numbers written to two decimal places, and two of these numbers summed to ten (see Table 1.1). The students' task was to find the two numbers that summed to ten in all of the 20 matrices, something that was impossible to do in the allocated time. Regardless of whether they solved all the matrices or not, the students were provided with 50 cents for each matrix they solved correctly.

Table 1.1   The matrices used in the study conducted by Gino and her colleagues contained 12 numbers written to two decimal places. Participants in the study were required to find the two numbers in the matrix that summed to ten

1.69	1.82	2.91
4.67	4.81	3.05
5.82	5.06	4.28
6.36	5.19	4.57

Source: Mazar, N., Amir, O., & Ariely, D. (2008). The dishonesty of honest people: A theory of self-concept maintenance. *Journal of Marketing Research*, 45(6), 633–644. Reprinted with permission, published by the American Marketing Association.

To provide a baseline, some of the students completed the assessment under normal test conditions. In a second scenario, a shredder was placed in the corner of the room, and participants were instructed to destroy their test paper prior to self-reporting the number of matrices they had solved correctly to the experimenter. As illustrated in Figure 1.3, participants in this scenario availed themselves of the opportunity to cheat and solved more matrices than the baseline group. In a third scenario, in addition to a shredder being placed in the room, a participant, who was an accomplice of the experimenters, stood up after one minute and clearly suggested they had cheated by announcing: "I've solved everything. What should I do?" After witnessing this, the level of cheating among the participants increased even further. In a final scenario that provided an interesting twist to the study, the third scenario was replicated except that the accomplice of the experimenters wore a t-shirt bearing the logo of a rival university. Under this scenario, the level of unethical behaviour decreased markedly.

Within organisations, everyone identifies with a group, be it their immediate team, a department, division or the entire organisation. We fail to recognise how the in-group favouritism this identification generates makes us more lenient when judging the behaviour of fellow group members. Behaviour that might be frowned upon when performed by a member of an out-group, could be endorsed and become an acceptable social norm for the group we belong to.

Recent research has also shown that simply reminding someone that they belong to a group that is characterised by immoral norms (in this case, the banking industry) can lead them to behave more dishonestly.[12] In this study, participants

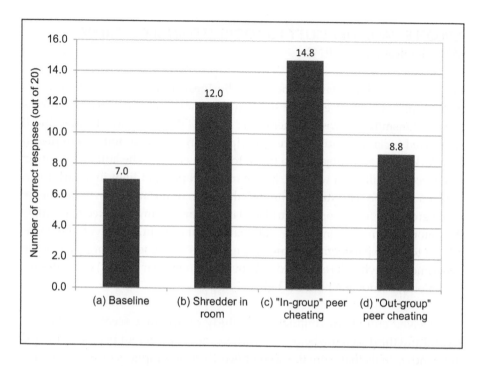

Figure 1.3   Performance of participants in an arithmetic task in the following four scenarios: (a) normal test conditions (baseline), (b) participants provided with the opportunity to cheat, (c) cheating modeled by a peer considered to be a member of the "in-group", and (d) cheating modeled by a peer considered to be a member of an "out-group"

Source: Gino, F., Ayal, S., & Ariely, D. (2009). Contagion and differentiation in unethical behavior: The effect of one bad apple on the barrel. *Psychological Science, 20*(3), 393–398.

were employees of a large international bank and took part in a coin-flipping game. They were required to self-report on the number of times they flipped a head (or tail) over ten consecutive flips. It was found that when the participants were reminded of their professional affiliation (bank employee), the level of mis-reporting increased. This result was not replicated when the study was conducted with employees of other industries, leading the authors to conclude:

> *Our results suggest that bank employees' compliance with the honesty norm was weakened in the professional identity condition.*

> *Our results suggest that the prevailing business culture in the banking industry favours dishonest behaviour and thus has contributed to the loss of the industry's reputation.*

3. PEOPLE HAVE THE ABILITY TO ADOPT SEEMINGLY EXTREME (AND IMMORAL) NORMS

Finally, and also important for the field of business ethics, is research that shows that people can adopt extreme social norms, and that these extreme norms can be transmitted across "generations". Mark MacNeil and Muzafer Sherif conducted a classic study where participants, in groups of four, were placed in a dark room and subjected to the autokinetic effect.[13] The autokinetic effect is a perceptual illusion where a stationary small point of light in a dark room appears to move. The study examined the types of norms that would emerge when groups of four people were placed in the dark room and asked to estimate the amount of movement in the stationary point of light. However, there was a twist to the experiment as some of the groups contained accomplices of the experimenters who were planted to provide extreme (far higher) estimates for the amount of movement in the light.

MacNeil and Sherif conducted the study under three scenarios, with the second and third scenario being those where the group of four people contained three individuals that were the accomplices. The accomplices in scenario three were instructed to provide more extreme estimates than those in scenario two. The results of the study showed that the naïve participants in scenarios two and three adopted the extreme estimates suggested by the planted individuals, such that the norms that emerged in these scenarios were much higher than the norms established in the first scenario where no accomplices were used.

Even more fascinating was that the experiment went on to investigate how social norms are transmitted by introducing "generational change". At the conclusion of each trial where the group had established a social norm for the amount of movement in the point of light, a participant was replaced. In scenarios two and three, the accomplices of the experimenters were the first to be removed, so that on the fourth trial, there were no accomplices remaining. As Figure 1.4 illustrates, the extreme norms established in these scenarios survived generational change. As naïve newcomers entered the groups, they embraced the previously established norms, with the less extreme norm in scenario two being stickier across subsequent trials. Although the norms in scenarios two and three did reduce over time, after eight trials they were still higher than the norm established by the groups that were never infiltrated by an accomplice.

In a real-life study that has parallels with the MacNeil and Sherif study, Lamar Pierce and Jason Snyder monitored the decisions made by inspectors working in the vehicle emissions testing market in a region of the US.[14]

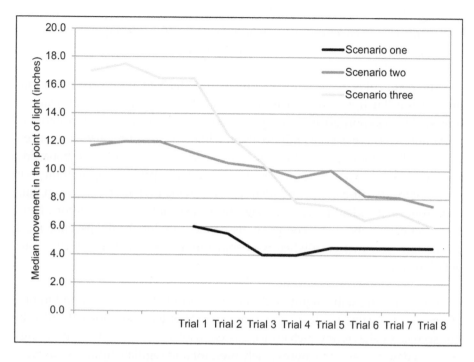

Figure 1.4 **Median light movement (in inches) established in each scenario across 11 trials. The final eight trials are those where there were no accomplices of the experimenters planted in any of the groups**

Source: MacNeil, M. K., & Sherif, M. (1976). Norm change over subject generations as a function of arbitrariness of prescribed norms. *Journal of Personality and Social Psychology, 34*(5), 762–773.

Although inspectors are legally required to follow strict testing procedures, there are considerable differences in the standards and practices adopted across facilities, with some displaying far more leniency than others – the potential for unethical behaviour is significant. Pierce and Snyder focused on inspectors who worked at multiple facilities, and investigated whether their standards varied as they changed employers. That is, like the participants in the MacNeil and Sherif study, how would these inspectors respond when they entered a "dark room" that contained existing social norms they may not necessarily agree with? They found evidence strongly suggesting that the ethical behaviour of inspectors shifted as they moved from one facility to another, and this shift could be explained by the organisational norms and ethics of their employer:

> When individuals work across different facilities, their behavior
> conforms to that of the facility that employs them. Our results suggest

inspector behavior converges toward the norms of the employer nearly immediately, with little lag or gradual adaptation.

The real genius of the study conducted by MacNeil and Sherif is that not only does it illustrate our capacity to adopt extreme norms, but it also shows how sticky these norms can be. People entering an environment where extreme or immoral norms exist can embrace them without being previously influenced by them. This does not mean that they do so willingly. Apart from bona fide psychopaths, of which there are very few, we all take pride in our morality – it is central to our self-concept and identity.[15] Behaving in immoral ways can thus compromise our identity, creating significant psychological discomfort. Leon Festinger coined the term "cognitive dissonance" to descibe the psychological discomfort we experience when we behave in a way that is contrary to our beliefs or values.[16]

When dealing with cognitive dissonance, people typically respond in one of two ways. Firstly, the dissonance may act to "bolster" their original belief. In this scenario, behaviour which is inconsistent with a person's beliefs and values creates a determination to more closely monitor and regulate future behaviour, ensuring that it doesn't compromise our standards.[17] Alternatively, dissonance may be addressed by changing one's underlying beliefs and values, making behaviour that previously may have been considered inappropriate or unethical suddenly acceptable. When navigating right versus wrong dilemmas, it is this latter approach which leads to undesirable outcomes.

Research has shown that this latter route to resolution of cognitive dissonance is more likely to be adopted when we are subtly persuaded to behave in a manner that is inconsistent with our beliefs and values. In a typical research paradigm illustrating this tendency, participants are asked to write an essay or give a speech on a topic that has personal relevance to them.[18] The participants must express a view that is against their beliefs, the only difference being that some are given no choice, while others are subtly persuaded to do so, making them feel like they chose to comply. It is this latter group that are more likely to change and align their beliefs with the counter attitudinal view expressed in their essay or speech. Humans have an uncanny ability to manipulate their beliefs, and justify behaviours and decisions they may have initially opposed. Social norms are just one of many mechanisms that can aid this shift, and many others are illustrated throughout this book.[19]

As my experience in the FX trading scandal at the NAB taught me, young people in particular are vulnerable to embracing and endorsing immoral social norms. As will be discussed in the following chapter when we explore the concept of ethical followership, it is rare that a young person entering the workforce for the first time would have taken the time to seriously consider and explore their values and what is important to them. Having not calibrated their moral compass, young people are more likely to use environmental cues to help them determine what type of behaviour is appropriate. As Michael Lewis rightly points out with reference to young people embarking on a career in finance, this can ultimately shape character:[20]

> The question I've always had about this army of young people with seemingly endless career options who wind up in finance is: What happens next to them? People like to think they have a "character", and that this character of theirs will endure, no matter the situation. It's not really so. People are vulnerable to the incentives of their environment, and often the best a person can do, if he wants to behave in a certain manner, is to choose carefully the environment that will go to work on his character.

The key insights provided by the above research into social norms has broad application to all of the well-known systemic ethical failures. Firstly, ethical failures are characterised by the emergence of descriptive norms that are at odds with the injunctive norms, and these norms work to drive and promote unethical behaviour. Secondly, as people become part of and identify with the groups responsible for the unethical behaviour, they tend to condone and embrace these descriptive norms, and at the extreme begin justifying behaviour they may have previously considered to be unethical. Finally, these descriptive norms can cause people to embrace conduct that may appear extreme to an outsider. Some real-life examples will help to illustrate.

In the FX trading scandal that engulfed the NAB, immoral social norms emerged that promoted excessive risk taking and misstating the true value of the currency options portfolio. For example, the investigation into the incident conducted by PricewaterhouseCoopers found, among other things, that:[21]

- "For a number of years the Traders misstated the profit and loss of the currency options desk using the practice of smoothing."

- "The VaR [risk] position records show that limits were persistently breached throughout 2003."

- " ... a large number of limit breaches were approved on a daily basis ... "

- "Multiple limit breaches were routinely signed off without rigorous investigation or actions taken to reduce positions."

The injunctive norms that existed at the time of the FX trading incident did not condone this type of behaviour – the NAB's 2003 annual report stated that "standards of ethical behaviour are reflected in our codes of conduct and our values".[22] However, as outlined above, in organisations where the descriptive norms are at odds with what the injunctive norms prescribe, the descriptive norms tend to prevail – what *is* done will override what *ought* to be done.

The LIBOR rate-fixing scandal was a systemic ethical failure that involved traders and brokers employed at a number of the world's largest financial institutions manipulating benchmark interest rates, primarily to enhance their own financial positions. In an article appearing in *The Economist*, the journal comments on the "everydayness" with which employees at major financial institutions manipulated the benchmark rates, and how they openly communicated and congratulated one another on their actions.[23] Once again, behaviour that is clearly at odds with injunctive norms and appears extreme to someone not in the "in-group" was normalised, and considered to be totally appropriate in that environment:

> In the rapidly spreading scandal of LIBOR (the London inter-bank offered rate) it is the very everydayness with which bank traders set about manipulating the most important figure in finance. They joked, or offered small favours. "Coffees will be coming your way," promised one trader in exchange for a fiddled number. "Dude. I owe you big time! … I'm opening a bottle of Bollinger," wrote another. One trader posted diary notes to himself so that he wouldn't forget to fiddle the numbers the next week. "Ask for High 6M Fix," he entered in his calendar, as he might have put "Buy milk".

In the world of professional cycling, drug taking was such a normalised activity through the 1990s and 2000s that cyclists not only spoke openly about when they were riding without the assistance of performance-enhancing drugs, but also developed their own vernacular for doing so. In the book *The Secret Race*, Tyler Hamilton talks about the first time he heard the term "riding paniagua" in the late 1990s:[24]

> It was around this time that I started hearing the phrase "riding paniagua". Sometimes it was delivered in a slightly depressed tone, as if the speaker were talking about riding a particularly slow and stubborn

donkey. "I might've finished higher but I was riding paniagua." Other times, it was mentioned as a point of pride. "I finished in the first group of thirty and I was paniagua." I came to discover that it was really [the Spanish phrase] pan y agua – "bread and water". From that, I made the obvious conclusion: Riding without chemical assistance in the pro peleton was so rare that it was worth pointing out.

Armed with this knowledge of social norms, let's now turn to an overview of the Stanford Prison Experiment. This study is arguably the most poignant illustration of how extreme and immoral social norms can emerge and be embraced by people of sound character, making them behave in totally uncharacteristic ways. Among other things, the experiment shows how the system within which an individual operates can have profound and perverse effects on their behaviour and character.

Stanford Prison Experiment

The bad apple-dispositional view ignores the apple barrel and its potentially corrupting situational impact of those within it.[25]

Philip Zimbardo, The Lucifer Effect

Of all the experiments conducted in psychology, the Stanford Prison Experiment arguably provides the most powerful illustration of how the environment within which one finds themselves can have a profound impact on their behaviour. In his book *The Lucifer Effect*, Philip Zimbardo, the man who designed and conducted the experiment, states:[26]

The primary simple lesson the Stanford Prison Experiment teaches is that situations matter. Social situations can have more profound effects on the behavior and mental functioning of individuals, groups, and national leaders than we might believe possible. Some situations can exert such powerful influence over us that we can be led to behave in ways we would not, could not, predict was possible in advance.

In recent times, the experiment has come under criticism. Among other things, the methodology employed by Zimbardo has been questioned, as has his subsequent interpretation of the results. In order to investigate the validity of the experiment and its findings, Alexander Haslam and Stephen Reicher conducted a replication of the study in 2001.[27] In what became known as the BBC (British Broadcasting Corporation) prison study (four one-hour long documentaries featuring the study were televised on the BBC in 2002), Haslam and Reicher found that although there are facets of the Stanford Prison Experiment that are questionable, there is absolute legitimacy behind some of the key conclusions:[28]

> *In general terms, we concur with ... Zimbardo and others that tyranny is a product of group processes, not individual pathology. Yet we disagree about the nature of these processes.*

One of the criticisms levelled at the Stanford Prison Experiment is that although the interpretations of the results would have you believe otherwise, not all of the participants allowed their behaviour to be shaped by the prevailing environment. In the experiment, as in life, there were people who, despite the behaviour and conduct of those surrounding them, somehow managed to not allow the situation to shape or compromise their morality. However, what is clear from both the Stanford Prison Experiment and its attempted replication some 30 years later is this: when people strongly identify with a group, then there is every likelihood they will internalise and embrace the norms and values associated with that group, regardless of how extreme they might be.

As the name suggests, the Stanford Prison Experiment involved building a prison in a basement corridor in the psychology building of Stanford University. Significant effort went into ensuring that the premises were as prison-like as possible. Laboratory rooms were converted into three small cells, with the original doors replaced by black doors with steel bars. A small unlighted closet became the solitary confinement facility. The participants were 22 male university students selected from a pool of 75 people who responded to an advertisement in a newspaper seeking volunteers for a psychological study of "prison life". To select the participants, the 75 respondents completed an extensive range of questionnaires which enabled the experimenters to build a comprehensive profile of their family history, physical and mental health, and propensities for antisocial behaviour, crime or violence. This process ensured that the 22 selected participants were as "normal" and "average" as possible.

After being selected for the experiment, the 22 participants were randomly assigned to the role of guard or prisoner. Undertaking a thorough selection process and then randomly assigning the participants to the roles of guard and prisoner was a crucial design element of the study. Not only did this ensure that the participants did not differ markedly from the "average" person in the population, but it also ensured that the behavioural patterns which emerged during the experiment were the result of the situation within which the participants were immersed in, not their underlying dispositions. As Philip Zimbardo states:[29]

> Systematic selection procedures ensured that everyone going into our prison was as normal, average, and healthy as possible and had no prior history of anti-social behavior, crime, or violence. Moreover, because they were college students, they were generally above average in intelligence, lower in prejudice, and more confident about their futures than their less educated peers. Then, by virtue of random assignment, the key to experimental research, these good people were randomly assigned to the role of guard or prisoner, regardless of whatever inclination they might have had to the other. Chance ruled.

Just as there was considerable attention to detail placed into the design of the prison, significant effort was also put into preparing the guards and the prisoners. The guards' orientation involved assisting with the final phases of completing the prison complex, and a briefing on what was required of them in their role. Although the briefing explicitly prohibited the use of physical punishment and aggression, they were provided with guidance on how they should carry out their roles, and told to "maintain the reasonable degree of order within the prison necessary for its effective functioning".[30] The guards' uniform consisted of plain khaki shirts and trousers, a whistle, wooden batons and reflecting sunglasses.

The participants assigned to the role of prisoner meanwhile were told to be at their place of residence the day prior to the experiment commencing. They were picked up and "arrested" by local police officers and processed as if they were an actual felon. Upon arriving at the simulated prison, the prisoners were stripped, sprayed with a delousing preparation and made to stand naked for a period of time before being provided with their uniform. An ID picture ("mug shot") of each prisoner was taken before they were placed in their cells. Their uniforms consisted of loose-fitting smocks with an identification number on the front and back, a light chain and lock around one ankle, rubber sandals and a cap made from a nylon stocking.

The effort that went into preparing both the prison and the participants not only ensured that the simulated environment was as realistic and authentic as possible, but also enabled the social norms surrounding prison life and the role of guards and prisoners to emerge as the participants immersed themselves in their roles.

What followed was as fascinating as it was shocking. Within hours of the experiment commencing, the guards, who were prohibited from using physical forms of punishment and aggression, began using "creative" forms of cruelty. Prisoner activities such as reading and watching movies were soon confiscated, and simple rights such as sleeping, talking with other prisoners, going to the toilet and eating became privileges which prisoners had to earn. Prisoners were routinely and arbitrarily subjected to "counts", where they were required to recite the rules and at times publicly humiliate their fellow "inmates". The guards became so immersed in their roles that many of them were shocked at their own behaviour when reflecting on it at the completion of the study. As one guard noted:[31]

> *I was surprised at myself ... I made them call each other names and clean out toilets with their bare hands. I practically considered the prisoners "cattle", and I kept thinking I have to watch out for them in case they try something.*

The spirit of the prisoners slowly crumbled as they became subject to sleep deprivation, humiliation and were made to beg for simple privileges. After expressing initial disbelief at their loss of privacy and treatment, the prisoners attempted a rebellion. When this collective action failed, prisoner cohesion broke down, and they became withdrawn, isolated and more willing to humiliate one another when asked to do so by the guards. Five of the prisoners were "released" within the first few days of the study as they began to show symptoms of acute anxiety and depression.

Prior to the study, the participants were selected and randomly assigned in such a way that minimal difference existed between the backgrounds and psychological make-up of the guards and prisoners. Within days of the experiment commencing, the differences between the two groups were stark. Although the experiment was scheduled to run for two weeks, it was prematurely terminated after just six days due to the deteriorating circumstances.

From a business ethics perspective, there are many valuable lessons to be taken from the Stanford Prison Experiment, but two in particular stand out. Firstly, it is a graphic illustration of how the situation can cause people of sound character to behave in totally uncharacteristic and inappropriate ways.

Environments can shape our character and morality, and provide a means by which we begin justifying and committing to behaviour we may have previously condemned. As explained at the beginning of this chapter, it highlights why any investigation into unethical behaviour must give proper consideration to the system within which the perpetrators of the unethical conduct operate. Attributing unethical behaviour to the misdeeds of a few "bad apples" or some "rogues", although intuitively appealing, may fail to address the issues that reside in a rotten system that fosters and endorses social norms promoting unethical conduct. Rotten systems will always override the most robust and rigorous of compliance frameworks.

With the benefit of hindsight, it was quite clear that during my time in the currency options business at the NAB, the situational forces at play made certain individuals (including myself) behave in ways which those closest to us would have considered to be totally out of character. We all, some of us more so than others, adopted the immoral social norms that emerged in the business. Furthermore, the group dynamics were such that there was extraordinary pressure to embrace these norms, a topic we will explore in greater detail in the following chapter. It is this backdrop that provides groups with a cult-like appearance – dysfunctional social norms and an insular group dynamic that gives group members little choice but to embrace the prevailing norms.

For a practitioner, the second lesson from the Stanford Prison Experiment is far more pertinent than the first, and that is the role of leadership. Leaders play a pivotal role in designing and maintaining the environment that fosters and promotes the unethical behaviour of the "bad apples". It is to this topic that we now turn.

The Role of Leadership

> *A leader is a person who has an unusual degree of power to create the conditions under which other people must live and move and have their being, conditions that can either be as illuminating as heaven or as shadowy as hell.*[32]

> *Parker Palmer,* Leading from Within

Another criticism that is often levelled at the Stanford Prison Experiment is that as the experimenter, Zimbardo played an active role in driving the behaviour of the participants. Experimenter intervention is one of the big taboos in scientific enquiry, as it can significantly bias and pollute the results. Zimbardo played the role of "superintendent" in the Stanford Prison Experiment, and provided guidance to the guards on how they should treat the prisoners. For example, in one of his briefings with the guards, he was reported to have said:[33]

> You can create in the prisoners ... a notion of arbitrariness, that their life is totally controlled by us, by the system, you, me – and they'll have no privacy ... We're going to take away their individuality in various ways. In general what all this leads to is a sense of powerlessness.

Although from a scientific perspective this level of intervention by an experimenter can be viewed as a legitimate flaw, from a business ethics perspective it is very instructive. What it illustrates is that leadership played a central role in creating a crucible that enabled some of the abhorrent behaviours witnessed in the Stanford Prison Experiment to emerge. This was not lost on Zimbardo:[34]

> The most important lesson to be derived from the SPE [Stanford Prison Experiment] is that Situations are created by Systems. Systems provide the institutional support, authority, and resources that allow Situations to operate as they do. After we have outlined all the situational features of the SPE, we discover that a key question is rarely posed: "Who or what made it happen that way?" Who had the power to design the behavioral setting and to maintain its operation in particular ways? Therefore, who should be held responsible for its consequences and outcomes? Who gets the credit for successes, and who is blamed for failures? The simple answer, in the case of the SPE is – me!

To determine who has the power to design the behavioural settings of a system and to maintain its operation in particular ways, one must look at where the power in the system resides. In their seminal paper titled *The Bases of Social Power*,[35] John French and Bertram Raven provide an analysis of the roots of power in groups and organisations. They proposed five bases of power, with a sixth subsequently added by Raven six years after the publication of the original paper. The six bases of power are:

- *Reward*: The ability to control the distribution of symbolic resources and rewards.

- *Coercive*: The capacity to threaten and punish non-compliant people.

- *Legitimate*: The right to require and demand obedience due to the authority that is sanctioned in certain roles.

- *Referent*: The ability to influence based on group members' attraction to and respect for the individual holding power.

- *Expert*: The perception that a particular individual has superior skills and abilities.

- *Informational*: The ability to control and disseminate informational resources.

People within groups or organisations who control these bases of power are more influential than those who are unable to secure a power base. In large organisations, these bases are typically controlled by the executive and select senior leaders. However, there are cases where leaders further down the chain of command are able to control a power base and be a centre of influence. The notion that the ethical culture of an organisation is shaped solely by the message emanating from the board and CEO is a little farfetched. Although there is no question that it begins with the "tone at the top", leaders at all levels of a large organisation can play a role in shaping the system.

Whatever the case may be, the majority of employees not in these pivotal roles within an organisation aspire to secure them. It is perhaps the lure of these roles that is the genesis of the phrase "the aphrodisiac of power", coined by former US Secretary of State Henry Kissinger. This lure has also been demonstrated in research which shows that people holding positions of power would rather incur an economic cost than relinquish them.[36] However, the joy and euphoria associated with successfully being appointed to one of these roles should be accompanied with a healthy dose of humility, as it is the people holding these positions who also have a disproportionate impact on the prevailing ethical climate of an organisation, sometimes in far more subtle ways than they appreciate. They are ultimately responsible for shaping the system that supports and fosters the behaviour within an organisation, ethical or otherwise.

As outlined by Ann Tenbrunsel and her colleagues, leaders within organisations can shape the system through the use of both formal and informal mechanisms.[37] Formal mechanisms are those that are documented and visible, such as codes of ethics, codes of conduct, training programmes, policies, procedures, formal communication, compliance and regulatory frameworks, and performance and reward frameworks. Apart from performance and reward frameworks which are discussed in chapter three, this book will not focus on formal mechanisms. This is not done to belittle their importance. Rather, the numerous ethical failures we witness proves that relying on formal mechanisms exclusively does not properly address the challenges associated with creating environments that promote ethical behaviour. Formal mechanisms are technical solutions that will only go so far in addressing an adaptive challenge – character and morality cannot be regulated.

Informal mechanisms meanwhile are the "subtle messages that are received regarding ethical norms, or what is 'really' appropriate from an ethical perspective."[38] Notice the parallels here with the concepts of injunctive and descriptive norms discussed earlier. Generally speaking, formal mechanisms communicate what *ought* to be done, and informal mechanisms communicate what *is* done. One of the key lessons for me emanating from the FX trading scandal at the NAB is the power and symbolism associated with informal mechanisms. Through their own actions and choices, the decisions they make, the decisions they fail to make, and the behaviour they choose to punish, reward, promote or ignore, leaders show their people not only what the organisation really values, but also the type of behaviour that is rewarded and gets you ahead.

Social learning theory provides an eloquent illustration of how people occupying the positions of power within an organisation can, through the use of informal mechanisms, play a central role in determining the types of social norms that emerge. Developed by one of the giants of modern psychology Albert Bandura, the theory represented a major contribution to the field of psychology.[39] Although a comprehensive review of social learning theory is not provided here, one of its most significant propositions is that in addition to acquiring knowledge and adapting behaviour through trial and error, people also learn by observing others.

According to social learning theory, we use credible role models, such as high-standing people in a status hierarchy who have the ability to control rewards, to help us determine what is acceptable and appropriate behaviour. The idea that ethical conduct can be learnt through role modelling is not new – the great Greek philosopher Aristotle stated that "the spirit of morality is awakened in the individual only through the witness and conduct of a moral person". However, Bandura was the first to begin providing experimental evidence of how the process of observational learning operates.

In a series of classic experiments using Bobo dolls, Bandura illustrated the conditions under which the aggressive behaviour of an adult role model was adopted and imitated by children. In one of these experiments, 72 children aged between three and six years of age were divided into three groups.[40] Each child viewed a video of an adult role model behaving aggressively towards a Bobo doll, with the video ending differently for each of the three groups. In the first group, children saw the adult role model being punished for behaving aggressively. In the second group, children saw the adult role model being rewarded, while in the third group, the video ended as soon as the adult role model had completed their aggressive behaviour towards the Bobo doll.

After watching the video, the children were placed in a room with many toys, including a Bobo doll. Half of the children were provided with an incentive to reproduce the adult's behaviour, while the other half were provided with no incentive. The question Bandura asked was, under what conditions would the children reproduce the aggressive behaviour of the adult role model they had observed?

The results, illustrated in Figure 1.5, show how both role modelling and the reward system play key roles in determining the behaviour of people within organisations. Firstly, and not surprisingly, the children who received an incentive to reproduce the adult role model's aggressive behaviour towards the Bobo doll behaved far more aggressively than the children who received no incentive. There is now ample evidence showing how reward systems can drive people to behave in inappropriate and unethical ways. As mentioned, we will visit this topic in chapter three, when we explore some of the factors within organisations that bring to the surface the less desirable qualities of the human condition.

More noteworthy, however, are the results from the children who were provided with no incentive. In this group, the children who witnessed the adult role model being rewarded for the aggressive behaviour towards the Bobo doll were far more likely to behave aggressively than those who witnessed the adult role model being punished. For the first time, Bandura was able to provide experimental evidence that humans can learn vicariously – although there was no incentive to reproduce the aggressive behaviour, the children nevertheless did so when they observed a role model being rewarded for that behaviour.

Just as the adults were the role models in Bandura's experiments, leaders that control the bases of power are the role models in large organisations. For these leaders there will inevitably appear some key moments where, through

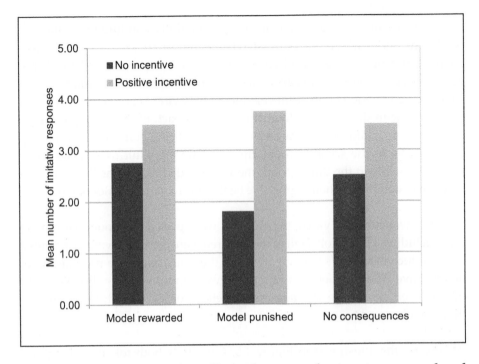

Figure 1.5   Average number of imitative aggressive responses reproduced
               by children after viewing an adult role model behaving
               aggressively towards a Bobo doll. The adult role model was
               either punished, rewarded or faced no consequences for their
               aggressive behaviour. Some of the children were offered
               rewards to reproduce the aggressive behaviour while others
               were offered no reward

Adapted from: Bandura, A. (1965). Influence of models' reinforcement contingencies
on the acquisition of imitative responses. *Journal of Personality and Social Psychology,*
1(6), 589–595.

their actions, choices and decisions, they will send powerful messages that
shape the ethical climate of their organisations and the types of social norms
that emerge. In the words of Joseph Badaracco, how a leader responds in these
"defining moments" shapes the "character of their companies":[41]

> *Defining moments for organizations, like those for individuals, can be
> subtle, quiet, and – examined one by one – seemingly inconsequential.
> Yet, whether managers intend it or not, their decisions and actions
> send continuous cumulative messages to their organizations about how
> things really work and about how to get ahead.*

*Defining moments shape an organization because they cut through all
of the finely crafted pronouncements about what the company aspires to
do and reveal instead what it actually does. These episodes set precedents
and create expectations that shape a company for years or even longer.
They define the purpose of the organization and at the same time how
the organization will pursue its purpose.*

This is why that, in addition to being moral people, ethical leaders
must be *moral managers*.[42] Moral managers devote a large portion of their
leadership agenda to ethics. They communicate a message of ethics and
values and ensure that their actions, choices and decisions visibly role model
this message. They use the reward system to hold employees accountable for
ethical conduct. This involves both disciplining employees responsible for
unethical behaviour, regardless of their status, tenor or reputation, and also
rewarding and promoting the ethical champions. It is this type of leadership
that enables the evolution of ethical cultures and increases the likelihood that
the conditions within the system encourage the emergence of moral social
norms that promote ethical conduct.

It is little wonder that research is beginning to emerge linking unethical
leadership to deviance and dishonest behaviour. In a recent laboratory study
conducted by Giovanna d'Adda and her colleagues, participants took part in
a die rolling game.[43] Participants were rewarded in such a way that it was in
their best interest to report that they rolled as high a number possible. After
rolling the die and reporting their performance, the participants were split into
groups of four people and one member of each group was randomly assigned
to the role of leader. These groups then took part in the same die rolling game
they had participated in as individuals. d'Adda and her colleagues found that
the groups who were more likely to misreport their performance in order to
maximise their reward were those led by participants who were dishonest and
misreported their performance in the first stage of the study.

Meanwhile, in a field study conducted by Lee Biggerstaff and his colleagues,
CEO ethicality was measured by whether they had engaged in backdating
stock options they had been granted as part of their remuneration package.[44]
Although in some cases the practice of backdating options is seen as legitimate,
it is generally undertaken in a clandestine way in order to increase executive
compensation at others' cost.[45] Using data from 1992 to 2009, Biggerstaff and
his colleagues identified 249 CEOs who engaged in this practice, providing
them with a sample of "suspect" firms. They then matched this sample with a

corresponding sample of firms from similar industries and of comparable size. Relative to the corresponding sample, the suspect firms were, among other things, more likely to engage in financial fraud, earnings manipulation and be the target of lawsuits.

For leaders presiding over an ethical failure, it is not enough for them to plead innocence on the basis that they were not personally involved in the unethical conduct, or for that matter, had no knowledge that it was occurring. Rather, the question they need to ask themselves is, given all of the available information, should they have known? Were there opportunities or moments, where through their decisions, choices, action or inaction, they sent signals that compromised the organisation's values and condoned unethical conduct? And in doing so, did they aid the creation of a system that became a crucible for immoral behaviour?

As mentioned earlier, the FX trading scandal at the NAB illustrated to me in no uncertain terms the power associated with informal mechanisms, and that despite being subtle, they can easily override the messages provided by the formal mechanisms. One could justifiably summarise the incident as a failure of leadership to act decisively in the defining moments and thus create the conditions in the system that would foster the emergence of appropriate social norms that promote ethical conduct. Leaders at a number of levels displayed behaviour and made decisions that were clearly not aligned with the organisation's values.

The PricewaterhouseCoopers investigation into the incident not only found that leaders failed to discipline the behaviour of the traders when it was clearly not aligned to the organisation's values, but they also failed to act when presented with evidence that provided them with the opportunity to do so:[46]

- "Warning signs received from the marketplace were ignored or not properly and independently investigated."

- "Although staff appraisals of the Traders contained adverse comments about excessive risk-taking, no effective steps were taken to constrain their behaviour."

- "No urgency was given to … the many breaches of limits by the currency options desk."

Also, in commenting on the culture that existed at the time of the incident, the report stated:

> *Meetings with staff and external third parties directly connected with the Traders reveal that the culture surrounding currency options provided the opportunity for the Traders to trade, incur losses, conceal those losses, and for them not to be detected despite warning signs. Some of the Traders treated aggressively anyone who questioned their activities …*
>
> *It appears that CIB [Corporate and Institutional Bank] and Markets Division management either allowed this culture to exist or took no action to prevent it insofar as it related to the currency options desk. Essentially this allowed the Traders to operate unchecked and flout the rules and standards of the bank.*
>
> *Ultimately, the Board and the CEO must accept responsibility for the "tone at the top" and the culture that exists in certain parts of the National.*

An analysis of most if not all of the well-publicised systemic ethical failures will find that they are littered with examples of how leadership at the most senior levels, through the use of informal mechanisms, failed to instil the conditions that promote the emergence of ethical environments within the organisations they lead. For example, in the LIBOR rate-fixing scandal, an investigation by the House of Commons Treasury Committee into the role played by Barclays Bank found that the incident could "not be dismissed as being only the behaviour of a small group of rogue traders":[47]

> *This attempted manipulation of LIBOR should not be dismissed as being only the behaviour of a small group of rogue traders. There was something deeply wrong with the culture of Barclays. Such behaviour would only be possible if the management of the bank turned a blind eye to the culture of the trading floor.*
>
> *The UK Corporate Governance Code is clear that "the board should set the company's values and standards". However, the misconduct of LIBOR and breakdown of trust with the regulatory authorities has demonstrated that the Barclays board has presided over a deeply flawed culture.*

In the aftermath of the financial crisis that caused global financial markets to go into meltdown and saw major economies across the world enter into a deep recession, the US government commissioned an investigation into the causes of the crisis. In delivering its findings, the panel conducting the inquiry concluded that the crisis was not caused by the actions of a few "bad actors", but rather by the inability of leaders holding key positions across the financial system to act appropriately when clear warning signs emerged:[48]

> Yet a crisis of this magnitude cannot be the work of a few bad actors, and such was not the case here. At the same time, the breadth of this crisis does not mean that "everyone is at fault"; many firms and individuals did not participate in the excesses that spawned disaster.

> We do place special responsibility with the public leaders charged with protecting our financial system, those entrusted to run our regulatory agencies, and the chief executives of companies whose failures drove us to crisis. These individuals sought and accepted positions of significant responsibility and obligation. Tone at the top does matter and, in this instance, we were let down. No one said "no".

> The captains of finance and the public stewards of our financial system ignored warnings and failed to question, understand, and manage evolving risks within a system essential to the well-being of the American public. Theirs was a big miss, not a stumble.

In the phone hacking scandal that rocked the media industry in the UK and appalled the public the industry informs, the role that leadership played at News International to create the conditions that promoted and fostered the unethical behaviour of their employees was questioned during the Leveson Inquiry. As the report produced by the inquiry stated:[49]

> The culture and tone of an organisation is set by and from the top:
> In terms of leading by example, insisting on adherence to standards,
> and implementing systems of governance which serve to identify and
> eliminate both legal and ethical risk at all levels of the organisation.

Although the report does not "comment in depth on the quality of leadership" at News International because doing so would "prejudice criminal trials", it did suggest that leadership, at the highest level of the organisation, had a central role to play in the scandal:

> *If News Corporation management, and in particular Rupert Murdoch, were aware of the allegations, it is obvious that action should have been taken to investigate them. If News Corporation were not aware of the allegations, which, as Rupert Murdoch has said, have cost the corporation many hundreds of millions of pounds, then there would appear to have been a significant failure in corporate governance and in particular in the effective identification and management of risks affecting NI [News International] and, thus, the corporation.*

Several senior figures at News International faced criminal charges over the affair. In June 2014, Andy Coulson, who was the Managing Editor of *News of the World* (the tabloid at the centre of the scandal), was found guilty of conspiracy to intercept voicemails.

In the Australian Wheat Board (AWB) oil-for-wheat scandal, the AWB was found to be paying "kickbacks" to the Iraqi regime in exchange for lucrative wheat contracts through a Jordanian registered transportation company. The scheme was in direct contravention to sanctions put in place under the United Nations Oil-for-Food Program established in 1995. In handing down the findings of the Royal Commission established to investigate the scheme, Commissioner Terence Cole made reference to the inability of leaders within AWB to establish a culture of "ethical dealing". More telling, he also made reference to how legislation, a formal mechanism, is unable to create or destroy such a culture – it is the responsibility of the board and management of companies to do so:[50]

> *At no time did AWB tell the Australian Government or the United Nations of its true arrangements with Iraq. And when inquiries were mounted into its activities it took all available measures to restrict and minimise disclosure of what had occurred. Necessarily, one asks, 'Why?'*

> *The answer is a closed culture of superiority and impregnability, of dominance and self-importance. Legislation cannot destroy such a culture or create a satisfactory one. That is the task of boards and the management of companies. The starting point is an ethical base. At AWB the Board and management failed to create, instil or maintain a culture of ethical dealing.*

An analysis of the widespread use of performance-enhancing drugs in professional cycling highlights a failure of leadership both among the cyclists and at the highest levels of the body governing the sport. The former head of cycling's governing body, Hein Verbruggen, appeared to turn a blind eye to the drug problems which plagued the sport, effectively providing tacit approval to the use of performance-enhancing drugs. In a documentary appearing on ABC Australia's *Four Corners* programme, Dick Pound, the former president of the World Anti-Doping Agency, recalled the response he received when he confronted Verbruggen about the problems that existed in the sport his organisation controlled and regulated. Here is a transcript from the documentary:[51]

> *I said "Hein, you guys have a huge problem in your sport". He said "what do you mean?" I said "the doping". "Well", he said, "that's really the fault of the spectators". And I said "I beg your pardon, it's the spectators' fault?" "Well" he said, "yes, if they were happy with the Tour de France at 25K [25 kilometers per hour], you know we'd be fine. But", he said, "if they want it at 41 and 42", he said, "the riders have to prepare". And I just shook my head and said "well, you heard it here first, you got a big problem".*

Lessons for Leaders

> *Example is not the main thing in influencing others. It is the only thing.*[52]
>
> *Albert Schweitzer,* Thoughts for Our Times

Of all the lessons provided to leaders by this chapter, two are pertinent. Firstly, we are all susceptible to behaving in uncharacteristic and, at times, unethical ways. The context within which one operates plays a pivotal role in determining how people respond and behave, and when one enters an environment where immoral social norms have emerged, it is often the case that their behaviour will align to these norms, regardless of their underlying character. It is for this reason that post-mortems of ethical failures must include a proper assessment of the system within which the unethical conduct occurs. Placing responsibility at the feet of a few "bad apples" or "rogues", although intuitively appealing, will more than likely fail to address far more deeper and significant issues in the system that drives the conduct of the people within it.

More importantly, however, the chapter has also highlighted how leadership plays a central role in creating a system that sustains immoral social norms and allows unethical behaviour to flourish. Through their own actions, inaction, choices, decision and the behvaiours they reward, discipline or ignore, leaders provide their followers with powerful messages on what is really valued and what is required to survive and succeed in an organisation. Although he was writing in a military context at the time, Simon Longstaff could not have put it more eloquently when he articulated the consequences of leaders failing to align their behaviours, choices and decisions to the values and principles their organisations espouse:[53]

> *Effective units depend on their leaders offering a shared sense of purpose and a framework of values and principles that motivate and guide – especially when the best laid plans have lost their coherence in the face of operational realities. However, it's almost impossible to build and sustain a functional ethos in circumstances in which leaders are thought to be hypocrites. Wherever hypocrisy is perceived, it generates cynicism which, like an acid, eats away at the ties that bind together communities and institutions.*

As a starting point, in addition to establishing a virtuous purpose, all organisations need to establish a code of ethics or other similar document.[54] Among other things, the code of ethics should articulate the core values and principles that guide the orgnaisation as they pursue their purpose. Of course, as symbolic as this document may be, it is by no means a "silver bullet" – it is up to the employees of the organisation to bring the document to life. More to the point, it is up to the leaders, the organisation's role models, to set the tone, and through their actions, choices and decisions, they must live and breathe the document.

As outlined earlier in the chapter, it is the descriptive norms that drive an organisation's culture, ethical or otherwise, and it is the leaders' responsibility to role model and establish standards of behaviour that align the descriptive norms to the injunctive norms. This is a lot easier said than done, and is especially difficult during challenging periods. It is during times of adversity, when the code of ethics calls for difficult decisions to be made and courageous conversations to be had, that the document's integrity is tested. The ability of leadership to send clear and unambiguous messages to their employees in these defining moments about the type of behaviour that is acceptable is arguably the best defence an organisation has against an ethical crisis.

Here are ten questions for senior leaders within any organisation to consider:

1.   Does your organisation have a code of ethics that articulates your organisation's core values?

2.   Do the organisation's leaders understand the values articulated in the code, and the types of behaviours that underpin these values?

3.   Does your behaviour send the right messages to your people by being consistently aligned to the organisation's values?

4.   Are there individuals in your organisation whose behaviours are not aligned with the organisation's values?

5.   If so, do you address this behaviour, or fail to deal with it and thus effectively compromise the code of ethics?

6.   Are you walking by behaviour within your organisation that should be condemned?

7.   What message are you sending by not acknowledging and addressing this behaviour?

8.   Are there individuals in your organisation whose reputation or status place them in a position where they are rarely challenged and are effectively "untouchable"?[55]

9.   Does the behaviour of these individuals make them worthy of this standing?

10.   Do you actively seek to reward and promote the "ethical champions" in your organisation in a symbolic way?

Where to Next?

Although this chapter has provided some insight into how context and systems evolve and promote unethical behaviour, several questions remain unanswered. For example, an organisation is ultimately a large group of individuals, and within this group exists many smaller groups and teams. When immoral social norms and the unethical behaviour associated with them emerge in organisations, not everyone aware of the behaviour is necessarily supportive of it. Furthermore, opportunities do exist for these people to question and challenge the behaviour. The normative approach to business ethics suggests that this is how they should respond.

However, immoral or unethical behaviour is not always challenged, suggesting that there are dynamics at play which make it difficult for people to question it and give voice to their disapproval. This is the topic we turn to in the next chapter – specifically, what are the dynamics at play that make it difficult for someone in a group to challenge their peers or their leaders when they witness behaviour they disapprove of? Where this chapter explored the contextual aspects of ethical scandals, the following chapter explores the relational aspect. As Donald Wargo and his colleagues point out, "ethics in the real world is often enacted as contextual and relational, carried out in the context of the institution or in relation to a superior or colleague."[56]

Notes

[1]   Kyi, A. S. S. (1991). *Freedom from fear*. Harmondsworth, Middlesex: Penguin Books.

[2]   Salancik, G. R., & Pfeffer, J. (1978). A social information processing approach to job attitudes and task design. *Administrative Science Quarterly, 23*(2), 224–253.

[3]   Reiner, R. (Director), Brown, D., Gilmore, W. S., Nicolaides, S., Pfeffer, R., Reiner, R., Scheinman, A., & Stott, J. (Producers). (1992). *A few good men* [Motion picture]. Los Angeles, CA: Columbia Pictures.

[4]   Cialdini, R. B., & Trost, M. R. (1998). Social influence: Social norms, conformity, and compliance. In D. T. Gilbert, S. T. Fiske, & G. Lindzey (Eds.), *Handbook of social psychology* (Vol. 2, pp. 151–192). New York, NY: McGraw-Hill.

[5]   See for example: Jacobson, R. P., Mortensen, C. R., & Cialdini, R. B. (2011). Bodies obliged and unbound: Differentiated response tendencies for injunctive and descriptive social norms. *Journal of Personality and Social Psychology, 100*(3), 433–448; Melnyk, V., van Herpen, E., Fischer, A. R. H., & van Trijp, H. C. M. (2013). Regulatory fit effects for injunctive versus descriptive social norms: Evidence from the promotion of sustainable products. *Marketing Letters, 24*(2), 191–203.

[6]   Cialdini, R. B., Reno, R. R., & Kallgren, C. A. (1990). A focus theory of normative conduct: Recycling the concept of norms to reduce littering in public places. *Journal of Personality and Social Psychology, 58*(6), 1015–1026.

[7]   Gunia, B. C., Wang, L., Huan, L., Wang, J., & Murnighan, J. K. (2012). Contemplation and conversation: Subtle influences on moral decision making. *Academy of Management Journal, 55*(1), 13–33.

[8]   Tajfel, H., & Turner, J. C. (1979). An integrative theory of intergroup conflict. In W. G. Austin & S. Worchel (Eds.), *The social psychology of intergroup relations* (pp. 33–47). Monterey, CA: Brooks Cole.

[9]   See for example: Tajfel, H., Billig, M. G., & Bundy, R. P. (1971). Social categorization and intergroup behaviour. *European Journal of Social Psychology, 1*(2), 149–178.

[10]   Gino, F., Ayal, S., & Ariely, D. (2009). Contagion and differentiation in unethical behavior: The effect of one bad apple on the barrel. *Psychological Science, 20*(3), 393–398.

[11]   This methodology was first devised and employed by: Mazar, N., Amir, O., & Ariely, D. (2008). The dishonesty of honest people: A theory of self-concept maintenance. *Journal of Marketing Research, 45*(6), 633–644.

[12]   Cohn, A., Fehr, E., & Maréchal, M. A. (2014). Business culture and dishonesty in the banking industry. *Nature, 516*(7529), 86–89.

[13]   MacNeil, M. K., & Sherif, M. (1976). Norm change over subject generations as a function of arbitrariness of prescribed norms. *Journal of Personality and Social Psychology, 34*(5), 762–773.

[14]   Pierce, L., & Snyder, J. (2008). Ethical spillovers in firms: Evidence from vehicle emissions testing. *Management Science, 54*(11), 1891–1903.

[15]   Aquino, K., & Reed, A. (2002). The self-importance of moral identity. *Journal of Personality and Social Psychology, 83*(6), 1423–1440.

[16]   Festinger, L. (1957). *A theory of cognitive dissonance*. Stanford, CA: Stanford University.

[17]   Shermin, S. J., & Gorkin, L. (1980). Attitude bolstering when behaviour is inconsistent with central attitudes. *Journal of Experimental Social Psychology, 16*(4), 388–403.

[18]   One of the earliest studies exploring the role freedom of choice plays in cognitive dissonance was conducted by Darwyn Linder and his colleagues: Linder, D. E., Cooper, J., & Jones, E. E. (1967). Decision freedom as a determinant of the role of incentive magnitude in attitude change. *Journal of Personality and Social Psychology, 6*(3), 245–254.

[19]   Recently, Rachel Barkan and her colleagues proposed that "ethical dissonance" is a special category of cognitive dissonance that can drive its own unique set of behaviours: Barkan, R., Ayal, S., Gino, F., & Ariely, D. (2012). The pot calling the kettle black: Distancing response to ethical dissonance. *Journal of Experimental Psychology: General, 14*(4), 757–773.

[20] Lewis, M. (2014, September 24). Occupational hazards of working on Wall Street. *Bloomberg View*. Retrieved December 15, 2015, from http://www.bloombergview.com/articles/2014-09-24/occupational-hazards-of-working-on-wall-street

[21] PricewaterhouseCoopers. (2004, March 12). *Investigation into foreign exchange losses at the National Australia Bank*. Melbourne, Australia: Author.

[22] National Australia Bank (NAB). (2003). *Concise annual report 2003*. Retrieved December 15, 2015, from http://www.nab.com.au/NABGroup/archives/annual-reports/Annual-Report-2003.pdf

[23] The rotten heart of finance. (2012, July 7). *The Economist, 404*(8792), pp. 25–28.

[24] Hamilton, T., & Coyle, D. (2012). *The secret race*. New York, NY: Bantam Books.

[25] Zimbardo, P. (2007). *The Lucifer effect*. New York, NY: Random House.

[26] Zimbardo, P. (2007).

[27] Haslam, S. A., & Reicher, S. (2006). Stressing the group: Social identity and the unfolding dynamics of responses to stress. *Journal of Applied Psychology, 91*(5), 1037–1052.

[28] Haslam, S. A., & Reicher, S. (2005). The psychology of tyranny. *Scientific American Mind, 16*(3), 44–51.

[29] Zimbardo, P. (2007).

[30] Haney, C., Banks, C., & Zimbardo, P. (1973). Interpersonal dynamics in a simulated prison. *International Journal of Criminology and Penology, 1*, 69–97.

[31] Zimbardo, P. (2007).

[32] Palmer, P. J. (2000). *Let your life speak: Listening for the voice of vocation*. San Francisco, CA: John Wiley and Sons.

[33] Reicher, S., & Haslam, S. A. (2006). Tyranny revisited. *The Psychologist, 19*(3), 146–150.

[34] Zimbardo, P. (2007).

[35] French, J. R. P., Jr., & Raven, B. H. (1959). The bases of social power. In D. Cartwright (Ed.), *Studies in social power* (pp. 150–167). Ann Arbor, MI: Institute for Social Research.

[36] Fehr, E., Herz, H., & Wilkening, T. (2013). The lure of authority: Motivation and incentive effects of power. *American Economic Review, 103*(4), 1325–1359.

[37] Tenbrunsel, A. E., Smith-Crowe, K., & Umphress, E. E. (2003). Building houses on rocks: The role of the ethical infrastructure in organizations. *Social Justice Research, 16*(3), 285–307.

[38] Tenbrunsel, A. E., Smith-Crowe, K., & Umphress, E. E. (2003).

[39] Bandura, A. (1977). *Social learning theory*. Englewood Cliffs, NJ: Prentice-Hall.

[40] Bandura, A. (1965). Influence of models' reinforcement contingencies on the acquisition of imitative responses. *Journal of Personality and Social Psychology, 1*(6), 589–595.

[41] Badaracco, J. L. (1997). *Defining moments*. Boston, MA: Harvard Business Press.

[42] Treviño, L. K., Hartman, L. P., & Brown, M. (2000). Moral person and moral manager: How executives develop a reputation for ethical leadership. *California Management Review, 42*(4), 124–142.

[43] d'Adda, G., Darai, D., & Weber, R. A. (2014). *Do leaders affect ethical conduct?* (Working Paper No. 167). Zurich, Switzerland: University of Zurich, Department of Economics. Retrieved December 15, 2015, from http://ssrn.com/abstract=2469782

[44] Biggerstaff, L., Cicero, D. C., & Puckett, A. (2015). Suspect CEOs, unethical culture, and corporate misbehaviour. *Journal of Financial Economics, 117*(1), 98–121.

[45] Narayanan, M. P., & Seyhun, H. N. (2008). The dating game: Do managers designate option grant dates to increase their compensation? *Review of Financial Studies, 21*(5), 1907–1945.

[46] The following information is taken from: PricewaterhouseCoopers. (2004, March 12).

[47] House of Commons Treasury Committee. (2012, August). *Fixing LIBOR: Some preliminary findings*. Retrieved December 15, 2015, from http://www.publications.parliament.uk/pa/cm201213/cmselect/cmtreasy/481/481.pdf

[48] Financial Crisis Inquiry Commission (2011, February). *The financial crisis inquiry report*. Retrieved December 15, 2015, from http://www.gpo.gov/fdsys/pkg/GPO-FCIC/pdf/GPO-FCIC.pdf

[49] The following quotes are taken from: The Leveson Inquiry. (2012, November). *An inquiry into the culture, practices and ethics of the press: Volume II*, by the Right Honourable Lord Justice Leveson.

Retrieved December 15, 2015, from https://www.gov.uk/government/uploads/system/uploads/attachment_data/file/270941/0780_ii.pdf

[50] Royal Commission into the Australian Wheat Board Oil-for-Wheat Scandal. (2006). *Report of the inquiry into certain Australian companies in relation to the UN Oil-for-Food Programme*, by Commissioner T. R. H. Cole. Canberra, ACT: Australian Government Publishing Service.

[51] McDermott, Q. (Reporter), & Hichens, C. (Producer). (2012, October 15). The world according to Lance [Television documentary]. In S. Spencer (Executive producer), *Four corners*. Sydney, Australia: ABC Television.

[52] Schweitzer, A. (1975). *Thoughts for our time*. White Plains, NY: Peter Pauper Press.

[53] Longstaff, S. (2012, November 20). Doing the right thing is the right thing to do. *The Australian Strategic Policy Institute Blog*. Retrieved December 15, 2015, from http://www.aspistrategist.org.au/doing-the-right-thing-is-the-right-thing-to-do/

[54] As will be shown in chapter three, a purpose that sanctifies financial performance is far from virtuous.

[55] Or as the consulting firm Leading Teams ask, "Who are the custodians of the behavioural standards in your workplace?" Leading Teams call these individuals the "centres of influence".

[56] Wargo, D. T., Baglini, N. A., & Nelson, K. A. (2010). What neuroeconomics informs us about making real-world ethical decisions in organizations. In A. A. Stanton, M. Day, & I. M. Welpe (Eds.), *Neuroeconomics and the firm* (pp. 235–262). Cheltenham, UK: Edward Elgar.

2

Group Dynamics

Relational

*Madness is the exception in individuals
but the rule in groups.*

Friedrich Nietzsche, Beyond Good
and Evil

At some point in our lives, we have all
succumbed to the pressures associated with
group membership. In many cases, the way
our behaviour is shaped by being part of
a group is quite innocuous – we may have
dined at a restaurant we didn't necessarily
approve of, worn clothes that were not aligned to our fashion sense, or gone
to a movie that we would ordinarily avoid. In other cases, group membership
can drive us to behave in unethical ways. The dynamics at play that can drive
this latter outcome are of particular interest to the field of business ethics, as the
majority of decisions made in large organisations are made in groups. Whether
this involves formal groups such as the board, the executive, or a leadership
team at lower levels of the organisation, or informal groups such as a leader
approaching a colleague and seeking advice, it is very rare that an individual in
an organisation makes a unilateral decision without someone else being aware
of it. As Donelson Forsyth says, "nearly every ethics issue is a group-level one,
because ethics is such an interpersonal process."

Groups present a paradox. On the one hand, research has shown that when
working on a task in isolation, groups tend to outperform individuals. In the
seminal study of this nature conducted by Marjorie Shaw in 1932, groups of
four people and individuals were asked to solve the well-known missionary–
cannibal dilemma.[1] In this problem, three missionaries and three cannibals
are sitting on one side of the river and want to cross it using a boat that can
only hold two people at a time. All the missionaries and only one cannibal
can row, and for obvious reasons at no time can the cannibals outnumber the

missionaries. Shaw found that the groups generated more correct solutions than the individuals working alone, and generally displayed superior problem-solving skills.

As instructive as these findings from Shaw are, they dealt with a situation where there was no uncertainty or ambiguity (the cannibal dilemma asks for a closed-form solution), and the groups within the study were not required to engage or interact with other groups or individuals with competing priorities. When these types of elements are added, research has consistently shown that groups are not only more dishonest than individuals,[2] but also harbour less guilt about dishonest behaviour.[3] What's more, recent research undertaken by Nina Mazar and Pankaj Aggarwal showed that merely making people feel like they are part of a collective not only heightened their propensity to bribe, but made them feel less responsible when doing so.[4]

What is of most interest to the field of business ethics is the dynamics behind the development of the "group mind". Specifically, what makes unethical behaviour more prominent in groups? Why are members of groups susceptible to condoning and being party to behaviour that they initially may disapprove of? If someone within a group is aware of unethical behaviour and is experiencing cognitive dissonance, why don't they express their concerns, as the normative approach to business ethics would dictate?

In my experience at the NAB, dysfunctional group dynamics in the currency options business played a significant role in promoting the emergence and maintenance of immoral social norms and unethical behaviour. Furthermore, although I was not privy to the inner sanctum of the leadership teams that sat above the currency options business, I dare say that suboptimal dynamics was one of the reasons why they failed to respond as senior leaders should when presented with numerous opportunities to do so. As the previous chapter outlined, inappropriate and unethical behaviour, flagrant and persistent limit breaches, and excessive risk taking emerged as social norms in the currency options business. Although this warranted a strong response from senior leaders, none was forthcoming.

By once again drawing on the relevant research in psychology and applying it to my experience, this chapter explores the types of dynamics that can result in groups failing to address unethical behaviour as it emerges. The chapter begins with a review of how power operates in group settings by describing in some detail the classic experiments into obedience undertaken by Stanley Milgram. The chapter then looks at how group members can become bystanders, conform and adopt extreme views. We conclude by exploring the concept of ethical followership. By being aware of these dynamics and addressing their root causes, leaders can not only optimise group dynamics, but also reduce the likelihood of unethical conduct and significantly improve group performance.

Power and Obedience

> *The person who, with inner conviction, loathes stealing, killing, and assault may find himself performing these acts with relative ease when commanded by authority. Behaviour that is unthinkable in an individual who is acting on his own may be executed without hesitation when carried out under orders.*[5]
>
> *Stanley Milgram,* Obedience to Authority

In chapter one, we saw how people who hold positions of power within organisations have a disproportionate impact on dictating the types of social norms that emerge, and also shaping the system that supports these norms. In this chapter, we explore how people holding positions of power in a group setting can directly influence the behaviour of individuals within the group. We will devote a large proportion of this chapter to exploring this topic for three reasons. Firstly, the topic represents a natural extension of the material discussed in the previous chapter. Specifically, people look to leaders to provide guidance on what constitutes appropriate behaviour and, as the quote from Stanley Milgram above testifies, even the most heinous of actions can be seen to be appropriate if authority figures legitimise them. Secondly, power is a dominant force in all social interactions, and this is especially the case in the workplace where one's position in an organisation is defined by a status hierarchy. Finally, authority and obedience to it was a significant contributing factor to the rogue trading incident at the NAB.

To explore the topic, we will review in considerable detail a series of classic experiments conducted by Stanley Milgram while he worked as a psychologist at Yale University.[6] Conducted in the 1960s, the experiments graphically illustrate how people have a propensity to respond in an obedient manner when taking orders from authority figures. Moreover, the experiments show that when someone is operating under the instructions of an authority figure, there can be a shift in their sense of morality. As Milgram states:[7]

> *Although a person acting under authority performs actions that seem to violate standards of conscience, it would not be true to say that he*

loses his moral sense. Instead, it acquires a radically different focus. He
does not respond with a moral sentiment to the actions he performs.
Rather, his moral concern now shifts to a consideration of how well he
is living up to the expectations that authority has of him.

Milgram recruited participants for his research through an advertisement placed in a local paper calling on people to take part in "a scientific study of memory and learning". This approach ensured the participants came from a broad range of socioeconomic, ethnic and professional backgrounds. Upon arriving, each participant was brought into the laboratory by the experimenter, and accompanied by another participant who was an accomplice of the experimenter. The experimenter then assigned the two participants to the role of either "teacher" or "learner", but the process of assignment was rigged such that the naïve participant was always assigned to the role of teacher. The experimenter then took both participants into an adjacent room where the learner was strapped into an "electric chair". Before leaving the room, the experimenter stated that "Although the shocks can be extremely painful, they cause no permanent tissue damage."

The teacher was then taken to the "shock generator", a large instrument that contained a panel with 30 switches. Each switch was labelled with a voltage designation, ranging from 15 volts to 450 volts, with the voltage designation increasing by 15 volts for each switch. Furthermore, switches were categorised into groups of four, with each category being assigned a verbal designation ranging from "Slight Shock" and "Moderate Shock" for the first two categories, to "Danger: Severe Shock" and "XXX" for the final categories. When the teacher pressed a switch, a bright red light corresponding to the switch was illuminated and an electric buzzing sound was heard. In addition, a blue light labelled "Voltage Energizer" flashed, and the needle on the "Voltage Meter" swung to the right. Despite the appearance of authenticity, the shock generator was not capable of delivering any shocks to the learner.

The learning task required the teacher to read out a series of word pairs, and then repeat the first word followed by four other words. The learner had to select which of the four words was paired with the first word when it was originally presented. Each time the learner gave an incorrect response, the participant was told to administer an electric shock. Furthermore, the participant was instructed to increase the size of the shock administered by one level each time an incorrect response was provided. If the maximum level of 450 volts was reached, the participant was instructed to continue administering shocks at 450 volts, and the experiment was ended after three shocks were administered at this level.

If during the experiment the participant turned to the experimenter for advice on whether to continue, or expressed concern and refused to continue, the experimenter used the following sequence of "prods" to bring the participant back into line:

- *Prod one*: "Please continue" or "Please go on."

- *Prod two*: "The experiment requires that you continue."

- *Prod three*: "It is absolutely essential that you continue."

- *Prod four*: "You have no other choice, you must go on."

These prods were used sequentially, such that if prod one was unsuccessful, prod two was used and so on. If the participant refused to obey the experimenter after prod four was used, the experiment was terminated. The experimenter was firm, but never impolite, and as Milgram stated, at no stage did the experimenter act in a threatening way towards the participant to elicit obedience:[8]

> Our studies deal only with obedience that is willingly assumed in the absence of threat of any sort ... Whatever force authority exercises in this study is based on powers that the subject in some manner ascribes to it and not on any objective threat or availability of physical means of controlling the subject.

Just like the Stanford Prison Experiment, Milgram's obedience study has also received considerable criticism of late. What's more, there are also some parallels in the nature of the criticism – just like Zimbardo, Milgram is criticised for not accurately documenting the role of the experimenter in his study. In her book *Behind the Shock Machine*, Gina Perry detailed her findings from a comprehensive review of the Milgram obedience studies which involved analysing participants' accounts and reading Milgram's unpublished files and notebooks.[9] Among other things, Perry disputes Milgram's version of events of how the verbal prods were delivered. Instead of being delivered in a firm, innocuous manner, Perry claims that the experimenter improvised and at times bullied the participant. Although this definitely changes how the results should be interpreted (obedience versus coercion), it doesn't change the insights the results provide, something we will turn to shortly.

In all of the trials in the experiment, the learner, who as mentioned was an accomplice of the experimenter, provided approximately three incorrect responses to every correct response. A series of prerecorded protests and cries for assistance from the learner were incorporated into the experiment, and these were played back at predetermined shock levels. The first sign of discomfort was expressed at the 75 volt level, by a mild "grunt", and this was repeated at the 90 and 105 volt level. At the 120 volt level, the learner shouted to the experimenter that the shocks were becoming painful, followed by painful groans at the 135 volt level. At the 150 volt level, the learner pleaded with the experimenter to be let out of the "electric chair". Similar cries for help at increasing intensity were heard at each level up to 270 volts, at which point the cries for help became agonising screams. At 300 volts, the learner cried in desperation that he was no longer providing responses. At this point, the experimenter advised the participant that a null response should be treated as an incorrect response, and to continue administering shocks to the learner. After violent screams of anguish and protest at the 315 and 330 volt shock levels, the learner went silent.

Before presenting the results, it is worth asking yourself how you think you would respond if you were a participant in the study. Would you disobey the experimenter at any point, or would you continue administering shocks despite the learner's pleas and cries of anguish? Milgram surveyed psychiatrists, university students and a group of middle-class adults and elicited their views on how they felt they would respond. Every respondent said they would disobey the experimenter at some point, with the majority (over 70 per cent) saying they would end the experiment at the 150 volt level. None of the respondents felt that they would continue administering shocks to the maximum level of 450 volts.

As Milgram states when commenting on the predictions provided by these individuals, they grossly underestimated the situational forces at play during the experiment:[10]

> These subjects see their reactions flowing from empathy, compassion,
> and a sense of justice. They enunciate a conception of what is desirable
> and assume that action follows accordingly. But they show little insight
> into the web of forces that operate in a real social situation.

In chapter one, we discussed how as humans, we have a tendency to dismiss the overarching context, and instead use a dispositional approach to explain behaviour. This tendency, which Lee Ross labelled the fundamental attribution error,[11] is one of the main reasons why we grossly underestimate our capacity to behave unethically. We fail to properly appreciate the power of the situation, and its ability to shape how we respond.

The results, illustrated in Figure 2.1, are startling. Of the 40 participants, 25 delivered the maximum shock level of 450 volts. Eighty per cent or 32 of the participants continued to administer shocks up to the 270 volt level.

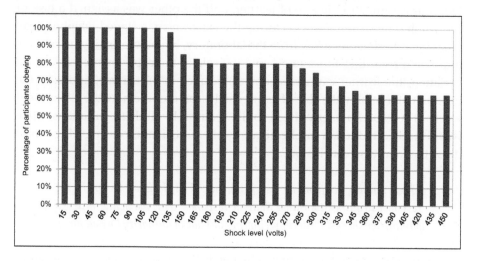

Figure 2.1   **Percentage of participants obeying the instructions of the experimenter at each shock level of the Milgram obedience studies**

Source: Milgram, S. (1974). Obedience to authority. New York, NY: Harper & Row.

Despite their obedience, it was clear that the participants experienced noticeable psychological distress, and attempted to deal with their dissonance using numerous techniques. For example, some participants read the word pairs out in a loud overpowering voice in an attempt to mask the learner's cries of anguish. Others pushed the switch down briefly, believing that doing so would reduce the intensity of the shock delivered. Meanwhile, other participants attempted to signal the correct response to the learner so that they would provide the correct answer. As Milgram states:[12]

> *A conflict develops between the deeply ingrained disposition not to harm others and the equaling compelling tendency to obey others who*

are in authority. The subject is quickly drawn into a dilemma, and the
presence of high tension points to the considerable strength of each of
the antagonistic vectors.

To confirm that it was the response to authority driving the observed behaviour of the participants and not some other factor, Milgram ran several variations of the study.[13] In one variation, despite his cries of anguish, it was the learner who pleaded for the experiment to continue, and the experimenter called for the experiment to be stopped. In another variation, the participant was joined by two accomplices of the experimenter when entering the laboratory. One was assigned to the role of learner, and the other was assigned a task of recording times using a clock. During the experiment, a rigged telephone call takes the experimenter away from the laboratory, but before exiting he asks the individual recording times to assume the role of the experimenter. In a third variation, the learner expresses some reluctance to participate, and asks the experimenter to play the role of learner so he can observe how the experiment works. The experimenter obliged to the request. In all these variations, there was a marked reduction in obedience by the participant, causing Milgram to draw the following conclusion:[14]

> *These studies confirm an essential fact: The decisive factor is the*
> *response to authority, rather than the response to the particular order to*
> *administer shocks. Orders originating outside of authority lose all force.*

More recent research conducted by Leigh Tost and her colleagues provides support to Milgram's conclusion that people tend to acquiesce to authority and not to orders.[15] In their study, groups worked together on a task that required them to solve a murder mystery. They found that when the group leader was made to feel powerful, they tended to verbally dominate the social interactions within the group, and decrease the extent to which other group members felt they were listened to and their perspectives valued. However, when the leader's formal position of authority was removed, although they still displayed the same autocratic tendencies, team members no longer displayed a willingness to defer or comply with the leader's dominant behaviour. This led the authors to conclude:

> *Thus, we found that the effects of subjective power on leader talking,*
> *team open communication, and team performance (both decision*
> *performance and learning performance) only emerged when leaders*
> *held a formal leadership role.*

The implications of the findings from the Milgrim obedience experiments for the field of business ethics are profound. As previously noted, power dynamics play a significant role in driving behaviour within the workplace, as one's position in an organisation is defined by a status hierarchy. Milgram showed that people will respond to the prompts of an authority figure that require them to behave in a highly questionable and unethical manner. He also showed how loyalty, so often trumpeted as a virtue in organisational life, is fatal when misplaced.

Even if, as Gina Perry claims, there was a degree of coercion or bullying in Milgram's study, this does not make the results any less relevant. As much as we would like to believe that it rarely occurs, situations do arise within workplaces where people fear there will be consequences associated with disobeying the instructions of an authority figure, even if the instructions require them to behave in a questionable manner. Under these circumstances, it would be easy to envisage how even a highly moral person would comply and behave in unethical ways. At the time of the FX trading incident at the NAB, there were consequences associated with failing to embrace the team ethos and aligning yourself with the prevailing social norms. When giving evidence in court, one of the junior traders recalled how a senior trader "had once warned her that a trader who had crossed him was now making bread for a living."[16] The ground was fertile for obedience to authority.

Indeed, excessive power is central to many of the well-known ethical failures in the business world. The case of the Ford Pinto is a classic illustration of this.[17] In the late 1960s, the Ford Motor Company was facing increasing competition from foreign imports. In response, the then vice president Lee Iacocca recommended they develop a compact car that would cost less than $2,000 USD to produce and weigh less than 2,000 pounds ("limits for 2,000"). The Ford Pinto rolled off the production line in 1971 and initial sales were strong. However, design flaws in the vehicle meant that the petrol tank was susceptible to ignition in a rear collision. Over 20 people were killed or injured as a result of these design flaws before a product recall was eventually ordered. In 1981, a court found the Ford Motor Company liable for the death of Lily Gray in May 1972. Gray was travelling in a Pinto that ignited after being involved in an accident.

In an explosive article that appeared in the *Mother Jones* magazine in 1977, it was alleged that the Ford Motor Company was aware of the design flaws.[18] Most controversial was the revelation that Ford had developed a fix at a cost of

$11 USD per vehicle. A decision was made not to implement the safer product design on the basis of a cost/benefit analysis. This analysis placed a monetary value of just over $200,000 USD on a human life.

Like all ethical failures, explanations for the Ford Pinto case are not straightforward – they are complex and multidimensional. However, power definitely played a central role. When an engineer who worked on the Pinto was asked if anyone advised Iacocca of the design flaws when they were discovered, he responded as follows:[19]

> Hell no. That person would have been fired. Safety wasn't a popular subject around Ford in those days. With Lee it was taboo. Whenever a problem was raised that meant a delay on the Pinto, Lee would chomp on his cigar, look out the window and say "Read the product objectives and get back to work".

A further variation that Milgram applied to his obedience experiments was to introduce a group paradigm. Where the initial experiments involved the teacher receiving instructions from the experimenter and acting alone, Milgram wanted to investigate what would occur if the teacher was placed in a group. That is, how would the behaviour of the teacher be influenced by the actions of their peers? This variation has significant practical importance because, as stated earlier, the majority of decisions in an organisation are made in a group setting. Before discussing the results from this iteration of the study, we will explore other dynamics apart from obedience that can lead to people in groups not only failing to voice their disapproval to questionable behaviour, but also embracing the behaviour and behaving unethically themselves. Two of these, the bystander effect and majority influence, are discussed next.

The (Innocent?) Bystander

> Bad men need nothing more to compass their ends, than that good men should look on and do nothing.
>
> John Stuart Mill, inaugural address delivered
> to the University of St. Andrews, 1867

Think of a time when you have been in a group setting, and someone has made a comment, performed an action or raised an issue that you take clear umbrage to. A mixture of emotions may have risen up within you – anxiety, anger or frustration. You feel like you should give voice to these emotions, but something stops you. You observe the reaction of your peers, but their silence and benign response make you feel like you are a lone voice, further rousing your inhibitions. Unbeknown to you, many of them are experiencing the same feelings and emotions as yourself. Psychologists have coined the phrase "pluralistic ignorance" to explain this situation, where the majority of group members reject a social norm or decision the group approves of, yet privately group members believe that the majority of their peers are in approval. It results in an illusion of unanimity being created.

Attributed to Floyd Allport,[20] the concept of pluralistic ignorance is not new, and is classically illustrated in the tale *The Emperor's New Clothes* by Hans Christian Andersen. It has parallels with the so-called "bystander effect", a concept classically illustrated in a series of experiments by Bibb Latane and John Darley.[21] Latane and Darley showed that people are less likely to respond to an emergency when they are in groups. In one of their experiments, participants were placed in a room that began to fill with smoke.[22] In trials when a participant was alone in the room, the smoke was reported on 75 per cent of the trials. When three participants were placed in the room, the smoke was only reported on 38 per cent of the trials. When a participant was placed in the room with two individuals that were accomplices of the experimenters who were told to acknowledge the smoke but then ignore it, the reporting rate dropped to 10 per cent.

Several processes have been used to explain this tendency for people in a group to remain silent when confronted with an emergency. These same processes can also provide plausible explanations for pluralistic ignorance, especially in cases involving ethical dilemmas where, like emergencies, we are dealing with ambiguous and uncertain situations. One of these processes is diffusion of responsibility, which simply states that the presence of others provides an individual with the ability to transfer their responsibility over to them. This results in them not feeling culpable despite their inaction. A second process is social influence, where an individual sees the passive and benign response of others as a sign that the situation may not be as serious as they perceive it to be. A final process at play is audience inhibition, where an individual chooses not to respond because they are self-conscious and fear they will look like a fool if they are overreacting – there is a desire to maintain their identity with the group.[23]

Research has shown that pluralistic ignorance does provide an explanation for an array of group behaviours, from whether students ask for assistance in a classroom setting[24] to the level of alcohol used on university campuses.[25]

However, there has been little research into the role pluralistic ignorance plays in group unethical behaviour. My personal experience suggests it plays a central role.

On several occasions during my time in the currency options business, members of the team, including myself, failed to voice their disapproval towards the inappropriate behaviour and immoral social norms that existed in the business, despite hindsight showing that their feelings were more broadly shared. This dynamic was possibly aided by the recruitment patterns of the business. Whether by design or accident, a preference was shown for hiring and grooming young trainees with no prior experience. As discussed in chapter one, having never explored the concept of values and morality in any detail, young, inexperienced employees are more likely to look to senior leaders for moral guidance when facing ethical dilemmas.

Inaction on behalf of the employees of the business, and for that matter the broader financial markets division, was yet another factor that provided a platform for immoral social norms to emerge in the currency options business. Over time, the majority of group members internalised these norms, and their attitudes and beliefs shifted accordingly. At this point, where the majority of group members embraced and committed themselves to the immoral social norms, majority influence emerged as a dynamic.

Majority Influence

> Whenever you find yourself on the side of the majority, it is time to pause and reflect.

> *Mark Twain*, Mark Twain's Notebook

Unlike pluralistic ignorance where the majority of a group's members privately disagree with the group, majority influence causes group members who disagree with the group to subsequently embrace the group's point of view because they are in the minority. This dynamic was classically illustrated in a series of experiments conducted by Solomon Asch in the 1950s.[26] Imagine you were a participant in the experiment. You enter a room and sit at a table with another six to eight people, and are advised that you are taking part in a study on visual acuity. You are shown two cards, similar to those illustrated in Figure 2.2.

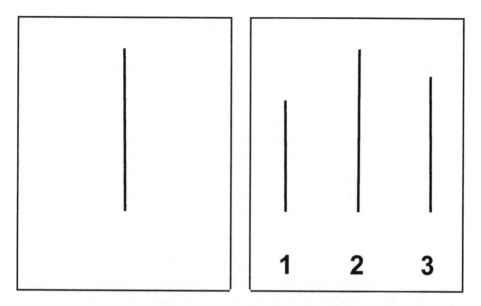

Figure 2.2   An example of the two cards that were shown to participants in the experiments conducted by Solomon Asch

Source: Asch, S. E. (1955). Opinions and social pressure. *Scientific American, 193*(5), 31–35. Reproduced with permission. Copyright © (1995) *Scientific American*, Inc. All rights reserved.

The first card contains a line that acts as a standard, and the second card contains three lines of different lengths. Your task is to nominate which line on the second card matches the length of the line on the first card.

There are a total of 18 trials, and in all trials the correct response appears self-evident. Each person at the table takes their turn to publicly nominate which line on the second card is identical to the standard, and you have been placed in a seat where you are always the last to announce your verdict. On six of the trials, all your fellow participants provide the correct response. However, on 12 of the trials, your fellow participants provide responses that are clearly incorrect. You are left in a position where your visual senses are clearly at odds with the unanimous opinion of the group. In this state of dissonance, how do you respond?

Unbeknown to you, all of your fellow participants are accomplices of the experimenter and the seating position was strategically arranged so that you are always the last to announce your response. Asch ran 18 trials with a total of 123 naïve participants. On over 36 per cent of the trials where the experimenter's accomplices made the incorrect selection, the participant succumbed to the influence of the majority. This is quite a significant result given there was absolutely no ambiguity surrounding which line on the second card matched the standard.

Several explanations have been proposed to account for this propensity of people to conform to majority opinion within a group. Recent research conducted by David Matz and Wendy Wood has shown that disagreeing with the majority can cause psychological discomfort in the form of cognitive dissonance.[27] Changing one's position so that it becomes aligned with the majority opinion is one way of reducing this dissonance. Meanwhile, Daniel Haun and his colleagues have shown that the tendency to conform to peers develops at a very young age, possibly suggesting an evolutionary basis for conformity.[28] Perhaps more telling is research suggesting that there is a biological predisposition to majority influence.[29] Using brain-imaging equipment and a modification of the Asch paradigm, Gregory Berns and his colleagues found that when participants agreed with the unanimous opinion of the group despite it being incorrect, there were changes to perceptual processing in the parietal cortex. Meanwhile, autonomous responses were associated with activity in the amygdala, a region of the brain involved in the experience of negative emotional states.

These types of findings suggest that there could be some automaticity associated with our tendency to succumb to majority opinion of the group. Suffice to say, as the study by MacNeil and Sherif described in chapter one demonstrated, people are prone to adopting the extreme views of the majority, especially when they are in ambiguous situations that require them to seek the guidance of fellow group members to form an opinion. Furthermore, if pluralistic ignorance can provide an explanation for how immoral social norms emerge, then majority influence can provide an explanation for how immoral social norms can become entrenched. This is especially the case when the immoral social norms are not only supported by the majority view of a group within an orgnaisation, but also by the actions, choices and decisions of the most senior leaders.

As mentioned earlier, one of the variations Milgram ran in his obedience experiments was to introduce a group paradigm. Milgram wanted to explore what impact the influence of group members would have on the actions of the participant, recognising that obedience differs to majority influence. The experiment proceeded as previously outlined, except on this occasion the participant entered the laboratory with the experimenter and three other individuals who were all accomplices of the experimenter. One of the three accomplices was assigned to the role of learner, while the other two were placed in a group with the participant. The group members were required to play the role of teachers and assigned to one of three roles: (1) reading the words that form part of the learning task to the learner, (2) informing the learner whether they have responded correctly, or (3) administering the shock by operating the shock generator. The naïve participant was always assigned to this latter role.

At the 150 volt level, when the learner made his first desperate plea to be released from the "electric chair", the teacher performing the word-reading role refused to take any further part in the experiment, despite the experimenter insisting that he continue. The experimenter then instructs the remaining two teachers to continue with the experiment, and in addition to his role of administering the electric shocks, the naïve participant is required to read the words that form part of the learning task. At the 210 volt level, the teacher who is playing the role of informing the learner of whether they have responded correctly also refused to participate any further, expressing his concern for the learner. The naïve participant, having witnessed the defiant actions of his two peers, is ordered to continue by the experimenter. How do they respond in the face of this majority influence?

Recall that in the original version of the experiment, where the participant acted alone under the instructions of the experimenter, 25 of the 40 participants administered the maximum shock of 450 volts. In this group paradigm where the participant witnessed the disobedient actions of their peers, only four of the 40 participants proceeded to administer the maximum shock. Of all the variations to Milgram's obedience experiment, none were as effective as this group scenario in reducing the obedience of the participant and diminishing the experimenter's authority. This finding led Milgram to draw the following conclusion:[30]

> When an individual wishes to stand in opposition to authority, he does best to find support for his position from others in his group. The mutual support provided by men for each other is the strongest bulwark we have against the excesses of authority.

We will return to this finding when we discuss ethical followership and whistleblowing later in the chapter. Before then, we will discuss one final group dynamic that arguably played a role in driving the extreme and unethical behaviour in the FX trading incident at the NAB, that being group polarisation.

Group Polarisation

When people are hearing echoes of their own voices, the consequence may be far more than support and reinforcement.[31]

Cass Sunstein, The Law of Group Polarization

The use of the word polarisation in "group polarisation" could be viewed as a slight misnomer, as polarisation in the usual use of the word refers to a split, or the manifestation of two contrasting views. However, group polarisation refers to a situation where group deliberation results in a collective view or opinion that is more extreme than what existed prior to the deliberations commencing.

Although the term group polarisation emerged in the late 1960s, its genesis as a theory began earlier in the same decade. In 1961, a student at Massachusetts Institute of Technology named James Stoner published a master's thesis that identified what became known as the "risky-shift" phenomenon. His research involved asking groups of six people to assess a variety of story problems known as "choice-dilemmas", an example of which follows:[32]

> *Mr. A, an electrical engineer, who is married and has one child, has been working for a large electronics corporation since graduating from college five years ago. He is assured of a lifetime job with a modest, though adequate, salary and liberal pension benefits upon retirement. On the other hand, it is very unlikely that his salary will increase much before he retires. While attending a convention, Mr. A is offered a job with a small, newly founded company which has a highly uncertain future. The new job would pay more to start and would offer the possibility of a share in the ownership if the company survived the competition of the larger firms.*

Participants are asked to advise Mr A by choosing one of a series of options that differ based on the probability of financial success for the newly founded company. In his research, Stoner found that the choices made by the individuals prior to commencing discussions within their groups were on average more risk averse than the choice arrived at after the groups had deliberated. Little did Stoner know that this risky-shift phenomenon he had identified was a special case of a more general phenomenon that has become known as group polarisation, a term coined later in the decade by Serge Moscovici and his colleagues.[33]

There is now a large body of research supporting group polarisation. An early review of this research showed broad application of the phenomenon to a variety of circumstances ranging from ethical decisions, jury decisions, person perception, judgments and attitudes.[34] Research has also shown that under conditions where the initial group tendency is for a more cautious approach, a "cautious shift" can also be induced by group deliberation.

Relatively speaking, the members of the currency options business during the time of the FX trading scandal at the NAB had an aggressive risk appetite and a propensity for pushing boundaries. In of themselves, these are not negative attributes. However, as the theory of group polarisation predicts, when a collection of individuals with these attributes are put together, the result can be extreme. From a business ethics perspective, group polarisation shows that social homogeneity can be damaging when people with extreme views come together to make decisions on issues that have ethical consequence. It also illustrates one of the many benefits of diversity.

Several mechanisms have been proposed to explain group polarisation. Two that have gained prominence are interpersonal comparison and informational influence. Interpersonal comparison suggests that polarisation is socially motivated. When people are exposed to the opinions of other group members, their strong desire to maintain their social standing within the group causes them to shift and adjust their position in the direction of the dominant position. Informational influence suggests that group discussion generates arguments that predominantly support the initial alternative of each individual, including some arguments that some group members may not have considered. This reinforcement of group members' initial opinions coupled with the introduction of new arguments drives polarisation.

Although research linking the two concepts is not common,[35] the FX trading incident showed me that the concept of deindividuation also plays a role in group polarisation. Coined by Leon Festinger and his colleagues, the term "deindividuation" refers to a psychological state where an individual becomes "submerged in a group" making them "more free from restraints, less inhibited, and able to indulge in forms of behaviour in which, when alone, they would not indulge."[36] Essentially, the collective becomes so powerful that it can transform individuals within it, allowing them to escape the regulation of injunctive norms.

Philip Zimbardo, of Stanford Prison Experiment fame, expanded on the theory of deindividuation.[37] In addition to group membership providing members with a sense of anonymity and reduced responsibility, Zimbardo proposed that it can also result in an individual experiencing increased arousal and decreased self-awareness. According to Zimbardo, these factors combine to lower the threshold for expressing inhibited behaviour. These dynamics have real application in organisations where decisions are largely handed down by groups, providing the individuals within them with a degree of anonymity. So often we hear phrases like "the board has decided", "the executive has concluded" or "the leadership team would like to announce".

A classic study conducted by Edward Diener and his colleagues illustrates how deindividuation can reduce inhibitions and drive extreme behaviour.[38] The study involved observing the behaviour of children trick-or-treating during Halloween. Upon greeting the children at the front door, the female experimenter acted surprised, commented on their costumes and then told the children they could take one candy from a bowl placed on a table just inside the front door. The experimenter then excused herself explaining that she had to go and work in another room, allowing the children to help themselves. In addition to the bowl full of candies, the table also contained a bowl full of coins. During the study, the anonymity of the children was manipulated by having the experimenter (on some occasions) ask the children to provide their name and address. Therefore, in addition to there being instances where the children would arrive in groups or alone, there were also instances where the provision of personal details meant that they were no longer anonymous.

The experiment was aiming to determine under which conditions children would take extra candy or money (or both) after being instructed to only take one candy. The results, illustrated in Figure 2.3, were aligned to what the theory of deindividuation would predict. Firstly, children in groups were more likely to disobey the instructions of the experimenter, as were children whose identity remained anonymous. In addition, the effect of anonymity was far more pronounced when the children were in groups than when they were alone – the anonymity provided by group membership can drive more extreme and immoral behaviour. The experimenters also found a strong modelling effect, something we explored in chapter one when discussing Bandura's social learning theory. In groups where the first child to enter the house took more than one candy, subsequent children tended to follow this norm established by the leader.

Before proceeding to the lessons for leaders that emerge from this chapter, it would be remiss not to spend some time discussing the role that followers play in promoting ethical conduct within organisations. Although this book is written predominantly for leaders, most leaders play dual roles – leader of

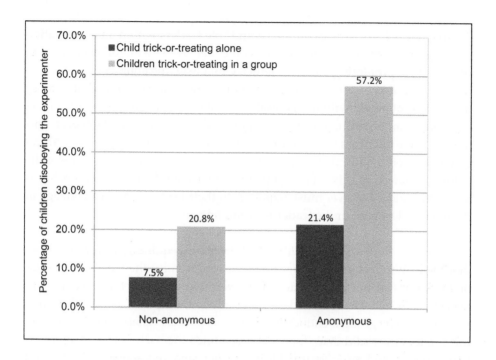

Figure 2.3   Percentage of children trick-or-treating in groups or alone who disobeyed the experimenter. Some children were required to identify themselves by providing personal details (non-anonymous) while others remained anonymous

Source: Diener, E., Fraser, S. C., Beaman, A. L., & Kelem, R. T. (1976). Effects of deindividuation variables on stealing among Halloween trick-or-treaters. *Journal of Personality and Social Psychology, 33*(2), 178–183.

their subordinates and follower to their leader. Therefore, they cannot neglect their role as followers.

Ethical Followership

> *Standing up for values is the defining feature of moral courage. But having values is different from living by values … moral courage lifts values from the theoretical to the practical and carries us beyond ethical reasoning into principled action. In the defining moments of our lives, values count for little without the willingness to put them into practice.*[39]

> *Rushworth Kidder,* Moral Courage

Although this book focuses on the central role leaders within an organisation play in shaping the behaviour of the people that serve them, followers too can play a role in promoting ethical conduct. Obviously, the ability of followers to do this is limited to some extent. As the previous chapter outlined, it is those in positions of power within organisations that have a disproportionate impact on shaping an environment that promotes ethical behaviour. However, this does not give followers the right to shirk their responsibility to promote ethical behaviour both within their teams and across an organisation. As some of the studies reviewed in this chapter illustrate, the leader–follower relationship is symbiotic, and a follower must acquiesce to their leader in order to engage in the unethical behaviour the leader is promoting.

It goes without saying that ethical followership requires followers to ensure that their own personal conduct does not compromise their personal values or the values of the organisation. Followers too, through their actions and behaviours, can act as role models, especially to their peers, as was illustrated when discussing group identification and social norms in chapter one. However, this is a lot easier said than done when one finds themselves in environments that promote and support unethical conduct, and the actions, choices and decisions of senior leaders ostensibly sanction this. It is because of the central role leaders play in promoting unethical behaviour that the most effective way followers can promote ethical conduct within their organisations is to encourage it in their leaders. Above all else, this is arguably the most important function of ethical followership.

To do this, followers must firstly provide their leaders with unequivocal support. The follower must not only support their leader in the pursuit of their organisation's purpose, but more importantly, in the pivotal role the leader plays in creating an ethical culture. Followers need to commend their leaders when their behaviour epitomises the organisation's values. They also need to support their leaders as they engage in the courageous conversations and make the difficult decisions that are par for the course when working towards creating an environment that promotes ethical conduct. As chapter one illustrated, by capitalising on the "defining moments", leaders can establish the conditions in the system that promote moral social norms and ethical conduct. Followers need to provide their leaders with the required support in these moments.

Secondly, and most importantly, followers can encourage ethical behaviour in their leaders by appropriately challenging them when the situation calls for it – followers too have defining moments. This is something that does not come naturally to followers because typically, followership is characterised by service, obedience and deference. However, when a leader's conduct is inappropriate, when a leader's decisions send a message that violates their own or the organisation's values, or when a leader fails to appropriately deal with the unethical conduct of an employee they are responsible for, then a follower must stand up and be prepared to provide honest feedback.

Challenging our leaders is no easy task. It is difficult because it places at risk our relationship with the leader and our standing within the team, creating conflict with our desire to identify with them. It is also difficult when working in a group with dysfunctional dynamics, that instead of encouraging open and honest feedback, demands loyalty to leaders who are poor role models, or conformity to a majority that has embraced immoral social norms. It is especially difficult in an organisation where the system supports and promotes unethical conduct. It is for these reasons that challenging leaders requires moral courage, because it involves giving voice to the dissonance we feel when a leader's actions violate our values and sense of what is right.

Although we all like to think we have the courage to challenge our leaders when the situation calls for it, research shows that we are poor predictors of our future behaviour.[40] This is especially the case when dealing with interpersonal encounters and conflict. One of the reasons put forward to explain our failure to accurately forecast how we will behave in these moments is (you guessed it) our inability to properly appreciate the situational forces that will be at play.

This was eloquently illustrated in a study conducted by Julie Woodzicka and Marianne LeFrance.[41] Female participants aged between 18 and 21 were asked to predict how they would respond if they were asked the following questions by a man in his early thirties at a job interview recruiting for a research assistant position:

- Do you have a boyfriend?

- Do people find you desirable?

- Do you think it is important for women to wear bras to work?

As expected, a majority of the participants said they would confront the interviewer, with 62 per cent saying they would tell the interviewer the questions were inappropriate or ask him why he asked the question, and 68 per cent indicating they would refuse to answer at least one of the questions.

When Woodzicka and LaFrance put a group of women in that same scenario in real life, none of the female participants refused to respond to the questions. While 36 per cent of the female interviewees politely asked why the questions were being asked, a majority of these only did so at the end of the interview.

If necessary, followers should consider consulting with colleagues and forming an alliance if challenging their leader unilaterally is proving difficult. As noted by Stanley Milgram as part of the findings from his famous obedience studies, "the mutual support provided by men for each other is the strongest bulwark we have against the excesses of authority". However, whether it is done alone or as part of an alliance, followers must remain supportive when challenging leaders. It should be done respectfully, preferably face to face, and in an affiliative manner, ensuring that it is the issue that is addressed and not the personality. It is always undertaken with the intention of supporting and upholding your core values and those of the organisation. In short, a follower must work hard to cultivate a relationship with their leader that is supportive at its core, and underpinned by courage, authenticity, honesty and candour.

Followers should not underestimate their ability to shape the behaviour of their leaders when they "speak truth to power". In a recent study conducted by Burak Oc and his colleagues, participants were required to distribute an endowment of 100 points they received each round (over ten rounds) between themselves and three "subordinates".[42] The amount of points accumulated by the participants determined the size of the monetary reward they received at the conclusion of the study. The participants were divided into two groups. In the "candid" group, participants received negative feedback from their subordinates when their distribution was not equitable. Participants in the "compliant" group meanwhile received positive feedback from their subordinates regardless of how the points were distributed. After receiving negative feedback, participants in the "candid" group responded by providing a more equitable distribution the following round. Furthermore, these participants also accumulated fewer points than participants in the "compliant" group, whose inequitable distribution of the points became more skewed and pronounced in their favour over successive rounds.

In some cases, despite a leader's conduct being clearly unethical, the prevailing social norms and group dynamic do not provide an environment where the follower can constructively and meaningfully challenge their leader, and any attempt to do so proves futile. In these circumstances, leaders lose their legitimacy, and the follower is left with no choice but to either leave the organisation or, in extreme cases, blow the whistle. Let me begin by saying that I don't envy anyone who finds themselves in a working environment where the prevailing social norms drive behaviour that is clearly unethical, and there is, or at least appears to be, tolerance, acceptance or endorsement of these behaviours by the leaders within the organisation. This is an incredibly difficult situation to navigate because, in effect, the organisation has failed you. Indeed, whistleblowers are only required when an organisation's leaders have failed to create an environment that not only promotes ethical behaviour, but encourages the surfacing of unethical conduct so that it can be properly managed and addressed prior to it degrading into a significant ethical incident.

There has been considerable research conducted in the area of whistleblowing. Unfortunately, given the difficulty associated with gaining access to actual whistlblowers and investigating the incidents in which they were involved, the research typically creates hypothetical scenarios and asks participants to report how they think they would respond should they find themselves in the scenario. In my mind, this method of enquiry severely compromises the validity of the research. Speaking from experience, no laboratory study could accurately recreate the circumstances I personally faced during my time in the currency options business at the NAB – facing the fork in the road in a hypothetical scenario is vastly different from facing it in reality. As the study conducted by Woodzicka and LeFrance illustrates, humans are notoriously poor at predicting how they will behave when facing an ethical dilemma.

I am also personally sceptical of other research into whistleblowing that focuses on ascertaining the types of personality or dispositional characteristics that may predict whether an observer of wrongdoing will take action and report it. Although some of this research may have merit, it is not surprising that it has also delivered inconsistent findings.[43] This line of enquiry fails to properly consider the power of the situation. As this book illustrates, the context a person finds themselves in plays an enormous role in determining how they will respond. Just like some situations can seduce people of sound character to behave in inappropriate ways, so too can situations encourage the most unlikely of people to respond in a prosocial manner when witnessing unethical conduct.

I am a case in point here. I had a fairly typical middle-class upbringing and was incredibly fortunate to grow up in an environment where my family, particularly my father, not only harboured virtuous values, but also set the most extraordinary example of how to live by them. Relatively speaking, I entered the workforce as a person with high moral character. Yet despite this, my moral standards were significantly compromised when I was placed in an environment where my sense of what was right and wrong was being challenged on a daily basis. My behaviour became aligned to many of the prevailing immoral social norms, as evidenced by the colourful language used in the taped phone conversations I was involved in and my knowledge of the practice of misstating the true value of the currency options portfolio. I was just as guilty as other members of the desk of laughing at tasteless jokes and encouraging inappropriate behaviour by not voicing my disapproval to it. Alas, I am no white knight.

I often get asked what it was that eventually drew my attention to my underlying values and moral obligations? For a number of reasons, making the decision to take a stand was incredibly difficult and, with the benefit of hindsight, I coped by distancing myself as much as possible from the unethical conduct in the business. This approach was convenient, because by distancing myself from the wrongdoing, I thought I also relinquished myself of the responsibilities and obligations associated with full knowledge. I was not displaying ethical followership – far from it. In the words of Margaret Heffernan, I was being willfully blind.[44] Maintaining an illusion spares you the anguish associated with having to make the tough choices, but at some point we all come to the realisation that in addition to providing us with the ability to choose how we respond, our free will also carries with it the burden of responsibility.

During a heated exchange with a senior trader, I was informed of the full extent of the losses being carried by the currency options business. At that point, I had no idea what to do with the information. After leaving work, I contacted a junior colleague, searching for guidance. Although she ended up playing a pivotal role in helping uncover the full extent of the losses, we were both none the wiser about what to do at the conclusion of our conversation. I went home and spoke to my wife, who I had always communicated with very openly about the circumstances and environment at work. She implored me to voice my concerns, even rallying the support of our neighbours to encourage me to do so. Yet despite her pleas, I was personally coming to the conclusion that my best option was to resign. I was displaying a preference for the path of least resistance.

In the office the following day, I opened up to a colleague who, over the preceding months, had taken it upon himself to play a mentoring role to me as he sensed I was struggling with the environment at work. I expressed my concerns to him, and said, "I don't know what to do." He asked me a simple question: "If you went into the system, could you find it?" I told him I probably could. His response was so simple yet so incredibly powerful: "You have no choice."

With those four words, my fate was sealed. He managed to draw my attention to my values and moral obligations in the most powerful of ways. Where before hearing those words there was fog and uncertainty, he provided absolute clarity. From that point on, I went into auto pilot, and I believe I have been in auto pilot ever since. I have faced the fork in the road and understand that, despite the associated tribulations, there is no substitute for taking the road less travelled.

Of the many lessons that can be taken from my experience, one is that moral courage is rarely the act of an individual acting alone. My willingness to open up and express my concerns to others enabled me to find allies who would ultimately provide me with the support required to stand up to authority. Without that support, I would have remained caught in a system that was unethical at its core and eroding my sense of morality. With their support, I was able to rediscover my values and remind myself of my moral obligations.

As stated, I don't envy anyone who finds themselves in a situation where the actions, choices and decisions of leaders are supporting an environment that is punctuated by unethical conduct, and any attempt to voice your concerns proves futile. One of the key pieces of advice I give to people in this predicament is to talk. Open up to as many people as you possibly can as not only will this help you reconcile with your values, but you may also find some unlikely allies. As Philip Zimbardo says, "heroism is a sociocentric not an egocentric response."

Recent research conducted by David Mayar and his colleagues seems to support the conclusions I draw from my personal experience.[45] Across two field and one laboratory studies, Mayar and his colleagues showed that the likelihood of unethical conduct being raised internally is significantly enhanced when in addition to having ethical leaders, people are surrounded by ethical co-workers and peers. What's more, this combination was also found to reduce the likelihood that participants would refuse to report wrongdoing on the basis that they feared retaliation or consequences for voicing their concerns. One cannot underestimate the courage one draws from supportive peers, or how difficult it is to cultivate moral courage when you are surrounded by immorality. As Mayar and his colleagues state, building a culture that promotes internal reporting "takes a village":

> Indeed, although ethical leaders want employees to report unethical conduct because it is simply the right thing to do, their efforts can fail if these employees do not believe their co-workers are ethical. Thus, employees must receive clear messages from leaders and from peers that reporting unethical conduct will be supported. This in turn suggests that "it takes a village", not merely an ethical leader, to encourage employees to report unethical conduct.

Lessons for Leaders

> Of all the passions the passion for the Inner Ring is the most skillful in making a man who is not yet a very bad man do very bad things.[46]

> C. S. Lewis, The Inner Ring

Arguably the biggest overarching driver of the group dynamics that have been explored in this chapter is our chronic need to belong.[47] The psychological literature is abundant with theories attempting to explain this primal human motivation to identify with and belong to a group. Although I will not dare attempt to do it justice here, there are some lines of enquiry in this area that are worth mentioning. In research conducted by Naomi Eisenberger and her colleagues, participants were excluded from a virtual ball-tossing game while sitting in a brain-imaging machine.[48] The results showed that the areas of the brain activated when the participants were excluded paralleled those that are activated when people experience physical pain. Being excluded from a group is painful.

In a more recent study conducted by Stefan Thau and his colleagues, some of the participants were instructed that a group vote had determined there was a high likelihood of them being excluded from the final of three group tasks.[49] After learning this, they had three minutes to solve ten anagrams that involved creating one word from a group of scrambled letters. The performance of their group in this activity would be measured against that of another group, and members of the winning group would receive a monetary reward. Unbeknown to participants, none of the anagrams had a correct solution, so anyone who reported having solved an anagram was being dishonest and inflating their level of performance. Thau and his colleagues found that the participants whose risk of exclusion was highest reported solving the most anagrams.

What's more, this pattern of results was strongest for participants who had a higher need for group inclusion. As the authors concluded, the need to belong drove dishonest behaviour in order to improve "inclusionary status".

These types of findings support the view that humans have a desire to form and maintain enduring interpersonal attachments and feel a sense of belonging. As Aristotle famously declared, "Man is by nature a social animal; an individual who is unsocial naturally and not accidently is either beneath our notice or more than human." This need to associate with and be accepted by others, although adaptive, can also be detrimental. It can cause us to obey the orders of authority figures that conflict with our values, even if the order is delivered in an innocuous and subtle way. It can result in us remaining silent when a group we are a member of is engaging in behaviour we believe to be inappropriate. It can drive us to adopt and embrace the view of the majority, even if we fundamentally disagree with it. Finally, it can result in us being party to a group that engages in behaviour that is far more extreme than what we would dare be associated with when acting alone.

All this being said, just like the leaders of organisations are well placed to shape a system and create an environment that promotes ethical behaviour, so too can the leaders of groups create a dynamic that is not dictated by power and ensures all voices are valued and heard. Not only will this type of dynamic reduce the likelihood of groups making inferior decisions, it will also act as a key defence against the emergence of unethical conduct. For this reason, creating optimal team dynamics should be one of the highest priorities for leaders.

A good starting point is to build a team containing individuals from diverse backgrounds. But even diversity of opinion and thought is futile if the group dynamic does not allow for its expression. Leaders must work hard at creating a dynamic that empowers group members, and allows them to express their views without fear or favour. To do this, there must first and foremost be a clear understanding within the group of the organisation's values and associated behavioural expectations. The harder work involves breaking down dysfunctional dynamics and creating an environment that fosters candour and honesty. An environment where group members hold one another accountable to the behavioural standards, regardless of their reputations, status or tenor. An environment where open and honest feedback is delivered regularly, and in a respectful manner. And an environment where conflict, instead of being avoided, is fully embraced. Ultimately, the group dynamic should make the conversations that are considered "difficult" part of the normal discourse.

When a group member calls out inappropriate behaviour, leaders must acknowledge their concerns and respond appropriately. This can be difficult, especially when the behaviour is attributed to a group member of higher status, or perhaps the leader themselves – generally speaking, leaders don't respond well to challenge.[50] However, how the leader handles this situation will go a long way towards defining the group's destiny. Failing to appropriately address behaviour that is at odds with the organisation's values sends a clear message that the values are negotiable. Leaders must deal with these situations in a way that is symbolic and sends a clear message that the organisation's values are not up for sale. At the same time, they must do this in a way that does not compromise the willingness of followers to continue giving voice to their values in the future. This can be a difficult balancing act.

Arguably the biggest obstacle to creating optimal dynamics within a group is the leader themselves. It takes an enormous amount of maturity and humility for a leader to recognise that, despite being the anointed leader of a group, there are times when their conduct falls short of what is required and they must call on their followers to lead. When a leader recognises this, they are ready to begin providing their followers with the space they need to voice their disapproval to inappropriate conduct and speak truth to power, thus giving them every opportunity to fulfill their roles as ethical followers.

You will recall that in the study conducted by Leigh Tost and her colleagues, where groups worked together to solve a murder mystery, team members no longer displayed a willingness to defer or comply with their leader's dominant behaviour when the leader's formal authority was removed. In a different version of the study, Tost and her colleagues had groups of four people work on a task that required them to recommend a candidate for a chief financial officer position. Information about the shortlisted candidates was not equally shared between group members. Tost and her colleagues found that when the group leaders were made aware of (a) the important contributions that team members can make, and (b) the role they play in eliciting these contributions, team communication and performance improved. This simple intervention reduced the deleterious effect of power in groups and increased candour.

As Margaret Heffernan states, "Unanimous decisions are incomplete decisions, made when there was too much power in the room, too much obedience, and too much conformity. If only one decision is visible, look again."

Here are ten questions for senior leaders (and followers) within any organisation to consider:

1.   Do all the members of your group have a clear understanding of the organisation's code of ethics and core values?

2.   Do all the members of your group have a clear understanding of the behavioural expectations associated with the organisation's values?

3.   As a leader, have you created an environment within your team that promotes open and honest feedback, ensuring group members are appropriately challenged when their conduct is not aligned to these behaviours?

4.   If so, when was the last time your behaviours were challenged by a member of the group?

5.   Is there a member of your group who holds considerable power?

6.   If so, are there times when opinions or comments made by this individual are followed by an unhealthy silence?

7.   As a follower, have there been moments when you have felt an urge to voice your disapproval, but have failed to do so?

8.   If so, what does this say about the group dynamic?

9.   Are there powerful factions or coalitions in your group?

10.   Do these factions or coalitions create suboptimal dynamics by driving obedience or majority influence?

Where to Next?

In chapter one, we explained how systems can create an environment within organisations that promote, facilitate and at worst institutionalise unethical behaviour, and the central role leadership plays in building and supporting these systems. The actions, choices and decisions of leaders send powerful messages to employees about the type of behaviour that is valued and rewarded. This chapter has illustrated how even though leaders within organsiations operate in groups, the dynamics of these groups can create scenarios where the actions, choices and decisions of senior leaders, despite being inappropriate or unethical, can escape censure and also be supported by other group members. My belief is that despite not being provided with the deserved attention in post-mortems, these two chapters describe the elements that are at the core of most of the well publicised ethical failures we have witnessed in recent times.

In the following chapter, we move beyond the contextual and relational factors that can drive unethical behaviour, and begin discussing the personal. Specifically, we explore three factors that are ubiquitous in all organisations and play a role in all ethical failures in business – money, power and fear. By once again drawing on the relevant research in psychology, the chapter will show how these factors can bring out the worst in the human condition and reveal our flawed humanity.

Notes

[1] Shaw, M. E. (1932). A comparison of individuals and small groups in the rational solution of complex problems. *The American Journal of Psychology, 44*(3), 491–504. Also see: Missionaries and cannibals problem. Retrieved December 15, 2015, from http://en.wikipedia.org/wiki/Missionaries_and_cannibals_problem

[2] Cohen, T. R., Gunia, B. C., Kim-Jun, S. Y., & Murnighan, K. (2009). Do groups lie more than individuals? Honesty and deception as a function of strategic self-interest. *Journal of Experimental Social Psychology, 45*(6), 1321–1324; Conrads, J., Irlenbusch, B., Rilke, R. M., & Walkowitz, G. (2013). Lying and team incentives. *Journal of Economic Psychology, 34*, 1–7.

[3] Gino, F., Ayal, S., & Ariely, D. (2013). Self-serving altruism? The lure of unethical actions that benefit others. *Journal of Economic Behavior & Organization, 93*, 285–292.

[4] Mazar, N., & Aggarwal, P. (2011). Greasing the palm: Can collectivism promote bribery? *Psychological Science, 22*(7), 843–848.

[5] Milgram, S. (1974). *Obedience to authority.* New York, NY: Harper & Row.

[6] Milgram, S. (1974).

[7] Milgram, S. (1974).

[8]   Milgram, S. (1974).

[9]   Perry, G. (2012). *Behind the shock machine: The untold story of the notorious Milgram psychology experiments*. Scribe: Melbourne, Australia.

[10] Milgram, S. (1974).

[11] Ross, L. (1977). The intuitive psychologist and his shortcomings. In L. Berkowitz (Ed.), *Advances in experimental social psychology* (Vol. 10, pp. 174–220). New York, NY: Academic Press.

[12] Milgram, S. (1974).

[13] As recently outlined in an excellent review of the Milgram studies by Nick Haslam and his colleagues, a total of 22 variations to the baseline experiment outlined above were conducted: Haslam, N., Loughnan, S., & Perry, G. (2014). Meta-Milgram: An empirical synthesis of the obedience experiments. *PLoS One, 9*(4), e93927.

[14] Milgram, S. (1974).

[15] Tost, L. P., Gino, F., & Larrick, R. P. (2013). When power makes others speechless: The negative impact of leader power on team performance. *Academy of Management Journal, 56*(5), 1465–1486.

[16] Moncrief, M., & Miletic, D. (2006, July 1). Rogue NAB traders face their judgment day. *The Age*. Retrieved December 15, 2015, from http://www.theage.com.au/news/national/rogue-nab-traders-face-their-judgement-day/2006/06/30/1151174396143.html

[17] Birsch, D., & Fielder, J. H. (Eds.). (1994). *The Ford Pinto case: A study in applied ethics, business, and technology*. Albany, NY: State University of New York.

[18] Dowie, M. (1977, September/October). Pinto madness. *Mother Jones, 18*. Retrieved December 15, 2015, from http://www.motherjones.com/politics/1977/09/pinto-madness

[19] Dowie, M. (1977, September/October).

[20] Allport, F. H. (1924). *Social psychology*. Boston, MA: Houghton Mifflin.

[21] Latané, B., & Darley, J. M. (1970). *The unresponsive bystander: Why doesn't he help?* New York: NY: Appleton Century Crofts.

[22] Latané, B., & Darley, J. M. (1968). Group inhibition of bystander intervention in emergencies. *Journal of Personality and Social Psychology, 10*(3), 215–221.

[23] Note the parallels between this final process and social identity theory that was discussed in chapter one – when we identify with a group, we tend to display in-group favouritism and are more lenient when judging the inappropriate behaviour of fellow group members.

[24] Miller, D. T., & McFarland, C. (1987). Pluralistic ignorance: When similarity is interpreted as dissimilarity. *Journal of Personality and Social Psychology, 53*(2), 298–305.

[25] Prentice, D. A., & Miller, D. T. (1993). Pluralistic ignorance and alcohol use on campus: Some consequences of misperceiving the social norm. *Journal of Personality and Social Psychology, 64*(2), 243–256.

[26] Asch, S. E. (1955). Opinions and social pressure. *Scientific American, 193*(5), 31–35.

[27] Matz, D. C., & Wood, W. (2005). Cognitive dissonance in groups: The consequence of disagreement. *Journal of Personality and Social Psychology, 88*(1), 22–37.

[28] Haun, D. B. M., Rekers, Y., & Tomasello, M. (2014). Children conform to the behavior of peers; other great apes stick with what they know. *Psychological Science, 25*(12), 2160–2167.

[29] Berns, G. S., Chappelow, J., Zink, C. F., Pagnoni, G., Martin-Skurski, M. E., & Richards, J. (2005). Neurobiological correlates of social conformity and independence during mental rotation. *Biological Psychiatry, 58*(3), 245–253.

[30] Milgram, S. (1974).

[31] Sunstein, C. R. (2002). The law of group polarization. *Journal of Political Philosophy, 10*(2), 175–195.

[32] Group polarization. Retrieved December 15, 2015, from http://en.wikipedia.org/wiki/Group_polarization

[33] Moscovici, S., & Zavalloni, M. (1969). The group as a polarizer of attitudes. *Journal of Personality and Social Psychology, 12*(2), 125–135.

[34] Myers, D. G., & Lamm, H. (1976). The group polarization phenomenon. *Psychological Bulletin, 83*(4), 602–627.

[35] For a rare example see: Lee, E. J. (2007). Deindividuation effects on group polarization in computer-mediated communication: The role of group identification, public-self-awareness, and perceived argument quality. *Journal of Communication, 57*(2), 385–403.

[36]   Festinger, L., Pepitone, A., & Newcomb, T. (1952). Some consequences of de-individuation in a group. *The Journal of Abnormal and Social Psychology, 47*(2), 382–389.

[37]   Zimbardo, P. (1970). The human choice: Individuation, reason and order versus deindividuation, impulse and chaos. In W. J. Arnold & D. Levine (Eds.), *1969 Nebraska symposium on motivation* (pp. 237–307). Lincoln, NE: University of Nebraska Press.

[38]   Diener, E., Fraser, S. C., Beaman, A. L., & Kelem, R. T. (1976). Effects of deindividuation variables on stealing among Halloween trick-or-treaters. *Journal of Personality and Social Psychology, 33*(2), 178–183.

[39]   Kidder, R. (2005). *Moral courage*. New York, NY: HarperCollins Publishers.

[40]   Tenbrunsel, A. E., Diekmann, K. A., Wade-Benzoni, K. A., & Bazerman, M. H. (2010). The ethical mirage: A temporal explanation as to why we aren't as ethical as we think we are. *Research in Organizational Behavior, 30*, 153–173.

[41]   Woodzicka, J. A., & LeFrance, M. (2001). Real versus imagined gender harassment. *Journal of Social Issues, 57*(1), 15–30.

[42]   Oc, B., Bashshur, M. R., & Moore, C. (2015). Speaking truth to power: The effect of candid feedback on how individuals with power allocate resources. *Journal of Applied Psychology, 100*(2), 450–463.

[43]   Vadera, A. K., Aguilera, R. V., & Caza, B. B. (2009). Making sense of whistle-blowing's antecedents: Learning from research on identity and ethics programs. *Business Ethics Quarterly, 19*(4), 553–586.

[44]   Heffernan, M. (2011). *Willful blindness: Why we ignore the obvious at our peril*. New York, NY: Walker Publishing Company.

[45]   Mayer, D. M., Nurmohamed, S., Treviño, L. K., Shapiro, D. L., & Schminke, M. (2013). Encouraging employees to report unethical conduct internally: It takes a village. *Organizational Behavior and Human Decision Processes, 121*(1), 89–103.

[46]   Lewis, C. S. (1944). *The inner ring*. Memorial lecture at King's College, University of London, London, U.K. Retrieved December 15, 2015, from http://www.lewissociety.org/innerring.php

[47]   Baumeister, R. F., & Leary, M. R. (1995). The need to belong: Desire for interpersonal attachments as a fundamental human motivation. *Psychological Bulletin, 117*(3), 497–529.

[48]   Eisenberger, N. I., Lieberman, M. D., & Williams, K. D. (2003). Does rejection hurt? An fMRI study of social exclusion. *Science, 302*(5643), 290–292.

[49]   Thau, S., Derfler-Rozin, R., Pitesa, M., Mitchell, M. S., & Pillutla, M. M. (2015). Unethical for the sake of the group: Risk of social exclusion and pro-group unethical behaviour. *Journal of Applied Psychology, 100*(1), 98–113.

[50]   Burris, E. R. (2012). The risks and rewards of speaking up: Managerial responses to employee voice. *Academy of Management Journal, 55*(4), 851–875.

3

Our Flawed Humanity

Personal

*Out of the crooked timber of humanity,
no straight thing was ever made.*

Immanuel Kant, Idea for a
Universal History from a
Cosmopolitan Point of View

As was highlighted in the introduction, the behavioural approach to business ethics attempts to address some of the shortcomings associated with the normative approach. Namely, where the normative approach operates on the premise that individuals are rational beings who understand the consequences associated with unethical conduct, the behavioural approach recognises that we are all fallible, and there are times when we behave unethically without even realising we are doing so. This is one of the core premises of this book – apart from some rare and extreme cases, there is no such thing as good and bad people. Rather, we are all capable of immoral behaviour.

This notion, that as humans we are all fundamentally flawed and capable of the greatest of goods and the most horrific of evils, is a central theme underpinning some of the greatest pieces of literature, art and film through the ages. A classic example of this is the epic poem "Paradise Lost" written by John Milton. In it, Milton recreates the scene from the Garden of Eden where Satan, disguised as a serpent, tempts Eve to eat from the Tree of Knowledge. It was at this point that paradise was lost and our compromised human nature was revealed.

In many ways, the title of this chapter is misleading. After all, chapters one and two have already illustrated how context and group dynamics can drive seemingly ethical people to behave in totally uncharacteristic, immoral ways. In this chapter however, we focus on three drivers at the heart of every ethical failure in the business world that have the ability to bring out the worst in the human condition. They are money, power and fear. Elements of these three drivers have already appeared in the previous two chapters. However in this chapter, we focus on addressing how the psychological experience of them can adversely influence a leader's behaviour. Money, power and fear play a significant role in driving human behaviour in a variety of, if not all settings. No book attempting to explain ethical failures in the business world would be complete without speaking to them.

All this being said, one should not conclude that money, power and fear are inherently evil and have no beneficial role to play in our organisations. Properly structured reward frameworks can motivate people to achieve beyond what they thought they were capable of. Power used properly can be used to bind and build. As Machiavelli famously said, "A man who has no position in society cannot even get a dog to bark at him." Finally, fear can alert us to potential threats to ourselves, our organisations and our communities, and ensure we respond appropriately. In the words of French philosopher Michel Foucault, "they are not bad, but they are potentially dangerous." Leaders must be aware of the potential dangers and understand how money, power and fear can drive immoral behaviour.

Before we begin, we will touch on a topic that has been debated for centuries and goes to the heart of explaining the human condition – whether humans are selfish, self-interested beings. After all, if the conclusion is that we are all innately self-interested creatures, then books like this that attempt to articulate the drivers of self-interested, immoral behaviour are rather pointless.

Are Humans Self-Interested?

I believe that every human mind feels pleasure in doing good to another.

Thomas Jefferson, letter to John Adams, 1816

For the majority of the past 300 years, the prevailing view among scholars and academics has been that humans are rational, selfish beings who are only interested in maximising their own profits (so-called *homo economicus*). The origins of this view of human nature can be traced as far back as the seventeenth century, when English philosopher Thomas Hobbes wrote, "Every man is presumed to seek what is good for himself naturally, and what is just, only for peace's sake, and accidentally." However, Adam Smith is often (and in my view undeservingly) credited as being the founding father of this so-called axiom of self-interest. In his book *An Inquiry into the Nature and Causes of the Wealth of Nations*, the Scottish philosopher and economist wrote:[1]

> *It is not from the benevolence of the butcher, the brewer, or the baker, that we expect our dinner, but from their regard to their own interest. We address ourselves, not to their humanity but to their self-love, and never talk to them of our own necessities but of their advantages.*

According to Smith, when an individual pursues their own self-interest in a free market, there are benefits to society as a whole such as innovation and competition. Smith coined the term "invisible hand" to describe this process.[2]

From a business ethics perspective, this rational, self-interested view of human nature means that the decision to behave honestly simply involves a trade off between the potential benefits (e.g. a monetary reward) and the associated costs (e.g. a fine). Therefore, if the authorities would like to reduce the incidence of unethical behaviour, they can do so by recalibrating the ratio between the benefits and costs. This typically involves increasing the likelihood of perpetrators being caught or increasing the magnitude of the punishment associated with the behaviour (or both).[3] When this occurs, the rational, self-interested human will recalibrate the costs associated with unethical behaviour, and, assuming they outweigh the benefits, adjust their behaviour accordingly.

However, over the past 20 to 30 years, we have begun witnessing a paradigm shift in this view of human nature. As mentioned in the introduction, the litany of ethical failures we have witnessed despite the heightened focus on regulation and compliance has played a small part in aiding this shift. More telling, however, is research in diverse fields such as psychology, neuroscience, sociology, anthropology, evolutionary biology, and behavioural and experimental economics that shows how when interacting with other people, humans do not necessarily operate in a way that seeks to maximise their own gains. Rather, this research suggests that humans care about fairness, altruism and reciprocity, and show a willingness to punish people who behave in a self-interested manner while rewarding those who do not. In the paragraphs that follow, we will review a very small sample of this research.

EXPERIMENTAL ECONOMICS

Over the past 50 years, there has been a proliferation of research in the field of economics using so-called social dilemma games. These games typically require players to make decisions that are either mutually beneficial or conversely benefit them at the expense of other participants. One of the simplest versions of these games is the Ultimatum Game, first proposed by Ariel Rubinstein.[4] The Ultimatum Game involves two players, one playing the role of the "proposer" and the other playing the role of the "responder". The proposer is provided with a fixed sum of money that must be shared between the two players, and they make a proposal on how it is to be split. The responder, who is fully aware of the total amount of money available, then decides whether to accept or reject the proposer's offer. If the responder accepts, the money is split as proposed and the game ends. If, however, the responder rejects the offer, then both players walk away empty handed.

If humans were rational, profit-maximising beings as suggested by the axiom of self-interest, then a responder in the Ultimatum Game would be happy with any proposal no matter how small as long as it is greater than zero, as this leaves them better off than what they were prior to the game commencing. Knowing this, a proposer would divide the sum of money in a way that would provide the responder with the smallest amount possible and keep the majority for themselves. However, across a range of studies, the proposer typically makes offers that provide 30 per cent to 40 per cent of the total to the responder, with 50:50 splits not being uncommon. What's more, when the responder is offered less than 20 per cent of the amount, the proposal is typically rejected.[5] Meanwhile, in a study conducted over 15 small scale societies that represented a large cross-section of economic and cultural conditions, Joseph Henrich and his colleagues found that although there was some variability in the results, the pattern was similar to that outlined above.[6] This led Henrich and his colleagues to conclude that "there is no society in which experimental behavior is consistent with the canonical model [of *homo economicus*]".

A less straightforward social dilemma game that has also been the subject of much research in the field of experimental economics is the classic Prisoner's Dilemma Game. The origin of the Prisoner's Dilemma Game can be traced back to the 1950s as part of a study into global nuclear conflict.[7] It requires two players to make a choice between cooperating or competing, with their respective payoffs determined by the combination of their responses. The payoffs are structured in such a way that the players are placed in a predicament as they must reconcile the tension between self-interest and the common good. As illustrated in Figure 3.1, assuming there are two players A and B, the payoffs follow a pattern as described below:

- If both players choose a cooperative response, they each receive a moderate payment.

- If both players choose a competitive response, they each receive a low payment.

- If one player chooses to cooperate while the other player chooses to compete, the cooperative player receives nothing and the competitive player receives a high payment.

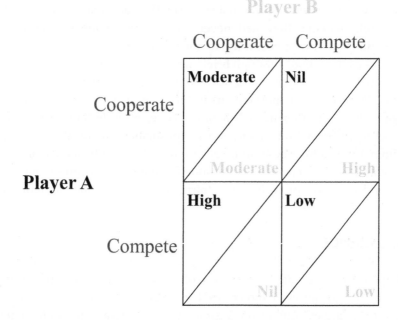

Figure 3.1   **The payoffs associated with the Prisoner's Dilemma Game**
Source: Adapted from: Roth, A. E. (1997). Introduction to experimental economics. In J. H. Kagel & A. E. Roth (Eds.), *Handbook of Experimental Economics* (pp. 3–108). Princeton, NJ: Princeton University Press.

As can be seen, there is an incentive for players to behave in a competitive manner, as doing this ensures they will receive a payment regardless of how their opponent responds (albeit that the payment will be low if the opponent also acts competitively). A cooperative response can result in zero payment if the opponent chooses to defect and act competitively.

Despite this, research has shown that in versions of the game where the players are not known to one another and participate on an anonymous basis, the cooperative response is chosen more than a third of the time.[8] What's more, even though it is in their best interest to compete, players have been found to cooperate over 60 per cent of the time when they are informed that their opponent has chosen to cooperate.[9] Similar results are found when the game is repeated and opponents develop a reputation for cooperation.[10] These results are once again at complete odds with what one would expect under the axiom of self-interest.

In a recent study conducted by Elliot Berkman and his colleagues, participants played both the Prisoner's Dilemma Game and the Ultimatum Game in two scenarios.[11] In the first scenario, the participants were randomly paired with someone they had never met before. In the second scenario, participants had the opportunity to meet and socialise with their fellow players. The interaction, although brief, made use of activities that enabled the participants to build rapport and develop intimate knowledge of one another. Among other things, the participants in this latter group were far more likely to cooperate in the Prisoner's Dilemma Game, provide larger offers as the proposer in the Ultimatum Game, and accept smaller offers as the responder in the Ultimatum Game. These findings support what will be a recurring theme in this chapter – when people are reminded of their social connectedness, their desire and capacity for reciprocity, fairness and cooperation is more likely to surface.

NEUROSCIENCE

In chapter two, we caught glimpses of how the field of neuroscience is providing insight into our innate need to belong. For example, research has shown that being excluded from a group activity activates the same region of the brain that becomes active when we experience physical pain. Furthermore, when we disagree with the majority view, the amygdala is activated, a region of the brain that processes negative emotional states. Neuroscientists have also shown that humans have a biological predisposition for cooperation, fairness and reciprocity. Typically, research in this area involves monitoring brain activity while participants are taking part in social dilemma games.

In one of the earlier studies adopting this methodology, James Rilling and his colleagues showed that mutual cooperation by players in the Prisoner's Dilemma Game was associated with increased activity in areas of the brain associated with reward processing.[12] The authors concluded:

> We propose that activation of this neural network positively reinforces
> reciprocal altruism, thereby motivating subjects to resist the temptation
> to selfishly accept but not reciprocate favors.

In a study adopting a modified version of the Prisoner's Dilemma Game, Doninique de Quervain and his colleagues provided a participant with the opportunity to punish their opponent when they chose not to respond cooperatively.[13] Not only did the participants display a willingness to punish, but doing so activated the reward regions of their brain. What's more, the greater the level of activity in the reward regions, the greater the cost a participant was willing to incur in order to punish their uncooperative opponent.

In a study using the Ultimatum Game, Golnaz Tabibnia and her colleagues showed that responders displayed increased activity in the brain's reward regions in response to fair proposals (i.e. proposals where the total money offered to the responder was greater than 45 per cent of the amount to be shared).[14] This was regardless of the monetary value of the offer. Meanwhile, the anterior insula, a region of the brain associated with negative emotions, was activated when a responder was considering an unfair proposal.

Finally, a biological predisposition to fairness has also been illustrated in a study that monitored our neurological response to inequality. Elizabeth Tricomi and her colleagues distributed monetary rewards to two participants after assigning them to a high or low-pay status.[15] As expected, low-pay participants showed greater neural activity in the reward region of the brain when they were the beneficiaries of monetary rewards. However, high-pay participants, despite stating a preference for monetary transfers to themselves, displayed greater activity in the reward region of their brains when monetary transfers were made to their low-pay counterpart. The authors concluded:

> *This apparent incongruity between stated behavioural ratings and brain data [for high-pay participants] indicates that basic reward structures in the brain may reflect even stronger equity considerations than is necessarily expressed or acted on at the behavioural level.*
>
> *Our results provide direct neurobiological evidence in support of the existence of inequality-averse social preferences in the human brain.*

EVOLUTIONARY BIOLOGY

Academics in the field of evolutionary biology are finding evidence for cooperation being one of the pillars of human evolution. In a recently published paper, Martin Nowak uses over 50 years of research to illustrate how five mechanisms have enabled cooperation to evolve among humans.[16]

These five mechanisms are kin selection (we favour cooperation with genetic relatives), direct reciprocity (we favour cooperation with individuals who we have repeated encounters with), indirect reciprocity (in order to enhance our reputations, we often behave altruistically to third parties even when they are not in a position to reciprocate), network reciprocity (by forming networks containing individuals who reciprocate, cooperators can prevail), and group selection (groups of cooperators tend to be more successful than groups of defectors). In the paper Nowak concludes:

> The two fundamental principles of evolution are mutation and natural selection. But evolution is constructive because of cooperation. New levels of organization evolve when the competing units on the lower level begin to cooperate. Cooperation allows specialization and thereby promotes biological diversity. Cooperation is the secret behind the open-endedness of the evolutionary process. Perhaps the most remarkable aspect of evolution is its ability to generate co-operation in a competitive world. Thus, we might add "natural cooperation" as a third fundamental principle of evolution beside mutation and natural selection.

Meanwhile, research by Sarah Brosnan and Frans de Waal has shown that even non-human primates respond adversely to inequality and display a sense of fairness.[17] In their study, two capuchin monkeys were required to provide the experimenter with a token in order to receive a food reward. Upon receipt of the token, the experimenter provided one of the monkeys with some cucumber and the other with a grape, the latter being more highly desired by capuchin monkeys. The monkeys receiving the cucumber responded adversely by not only refusing to eat the reward, but also refusing to participate any further in the experiment. In trials of the experiment where both monkeys were offered cucumber as the food reward, none of these responses was elicited. According to Brosnan and de Waal, "these reactions support an early evolutionary origin of inequity aversion."[18]

In sum, all of the above research paints a picture of human nature far different from the one suggested by the axiom of self-interest. There are times when we value fairness above maximising our own profits, when our emotions can cause us to behave in ways that are considered to be irrational, and when cooperation and reciprocity does dominate over self-interest. Obviously, the findings are not unequivocal – we do not behave in an altruistic, cooperative manner all the time in every circumstance. There are factors and contexts that can drive purely self-interested behaviour, as this book illustrates.

This being said, one should not underestimate the significance of the paradigm shift associated with the above findings. The frameworks that underpin our institutions have all been developed on the basis that we operate as *homo economicus* dictates, a model that has significant shortcomings. As Matthew Lieberman outlines, this approach can result in suboptimal outcomes:[19]

> Because real insight into our social nature has gained momentum only in the last few decades, there are tremendous inefficiencies in how institutions and organizations operate. Societal institutions are founded, implicitly or explicitly, on a worldview of how humans function. These are theories regarding the gears and levers or our nature that institutions try to operate on in order to strengthen society. Our schools, companies, sports teams, military, government, and health care institutions cannot reach their full potential while working from erroneous theories that characterize our social nature incorrectly.

This is worth keeping in mind as we turn to exploring money, a big driver of unethical behaviour in our organisations, yet one that we can control through the performance and reward frameworks that we devise and employ in our institutions.

Money

> Eric: They told me they were going to drag me through hell on everything from my options to healthcare over the next two years or I come back and make ... (he looks up and does a little math in his head) $176,471.00 an hour to sit in this room quietly ... it wasn't much of a choice.
>
> Sarah: It never is.[20]

Scene 66, Margin Call

When we talk about how money influences behaviour within organisations, we are essentially talking about performance and reward. As mentioned in chapter one, performance and reward frameworks are one of the first levers that leaders reach for when trying to shape the system and environment within their organisations, and this topic could have legitimately belonged in that chapter. However, given the central role money plays in ethical scandals and its ability to corrupt individuals and bring out the worst in the human condition, it is covered in this chapter alongside power and fear.

Performance and reward are two sides of the same coin – you can't address one without speaking to the other. Organisations typically establish benchmarks for performance. It is the ability of individuals to surpass these benchmarks that then determines reward, especially in organisations that use some sort of bonus scheme to reward their employees. As we will see, although inappropriately structured performance and reward frameworks can act as catalysts for unethical behaviour, an even larger concern is organisations that foster an obsessive focus on hitting benchmarks or chasing reward. Fostering a myopic pursuit of outcomes and monetary reward can come at detrimental ethical costs.

PERFORMANCE

> *Managers that always promise to "make the numbers" will at some*
> *point be tempted to make up the numbers.*[21]

> *Warren Buffett,* Warren Buffet's Management Secrets

It has long been established that specific, challenging performance benchmarks (or goals) lead to superior effort and performance when compared to abstract, vague goals such as "do your best". As stated by Edwin Locke and Gary Latham, "so long as a person is committed to the goal, has the requisite ability to attain it, and does not have conflicting goals, there is a positive, linear relationship between goal difficulty and task performance."[22] However, in some circumstances, performance benchmarks can drive inappropriate and unethical behaviour. One such circumstance is when they focus attention too narrowly, creating "tunnel vision", excessive pressure, and potentially driving an "at any cost" attitude. In these situations, the attainment of the goal can come at the cost of other considerations such as ethical conduct.

One of the most ingenious studies in psychology that illustrates how narrowly focusing our attention can cause us to be "blind" to other events in our environment was conducted by Daniel Simons and Christopher Chabris.[23] Based on similar studies conducted by Ulric Neisser and his colleagues some 20 years earlier,[24] Simons and Chabris created a video where two groups of three people each, one wearing white shirts and the other wearing black shirts, pass a ball to one another. Participants in the study are asked to watch the video and count the number of passes among people in each of the two teams. Approximately 45 seconds into the scene, a woman wearing a gorilla costume walks into the middle of the screen, pounds her chest, and then walks out of picture. Approximately half of the participants fail to notice the gorilla. This "blindness" is more pronounced for participants who were asked to count the number of passes among the team wearing white shirts.[25]

In a similar study illustrating the perils of narrowly focusing attention on a performance goal, Barry Staw and Richard Boettger asked participants to review a paragraph that was going to be used on a recruitment brochure for their university.[26] Compared to participants who were simply instructed to "do their best", participants that were asked to focus on correcting grammatical errors were far less likely to correct blatant content errors.

From a business ethics perspective, the findings from these types of studies illustrate the peril associated with a maniacal focus on specific performance goals. Indeed, many (if not all) of the well-publicised ethical failures in business are the result of appropriate conduct being neglected due to an obsessive, blinkered pursuit of performance goals and financial outcomes, creating environments where the ends justify the means. In the FX trading scandal at the NAB, the judge presiding over one of the court cases that followed the incident spoke to the "culture of profit-driven morality" that existed at the time of the scandal.[27]

While an obsessive focus on performance targets can drive inappropriate behaviour on its own, research has also shown that the use of financial incentives to motivate goal attainment acts to inflate the level of unethical conduct. In a study conducted by Steven Grover and Chun Hui, participants were placed into one of the following three groups: (a) a group with low-performance benchmarks, (b) a group with high-performance benchmarks, and (c) a group with both high-performance benchmarks and reward.[28] They then undertook a proofreading task, and anonymously self-reported their performance on both speed and accuracy. Unbeknown to the participants, the computer terminal they were using was also tracking and recording their performance. Although actual performance between the three groups did not differ, reported performance did. The results showed that the imposition of high-performance benchmarks caused participants to lie and report performance ratings higher than what was achieved. Furthermore, when reward was combined with high-performance benchmarks, the level of lying increased even further.

Research by Charles Cadsby and his colleagues meanwhile has shown that when financial incentives are used to motivate people to reach performance targets, how the incentive schemes are structured plays a role in determining whether they will engage in dishonest behaviour.[29] In their study, participants were asked to create as many words as possible in seven anagram tasks lasting one minute each. Participants' anonymity was protected in the study, thus providing them with the opportunity to cheat. They were divided into three groups based on the following reward structures:

- *Linear-Based Bonus*: A base payment of $3.00 and $0.40 for each correct word created.

- *Target-Based Bonus*: A base payment of $3.00 and $3.60 each time nine or more words were created.

- *Relative-Based Bonus*: A base payment of $3.00 and $3.60 each time their performance was at or above the 85th percentile.

Target-based bonus schemes are commonly used in the banking and finance industry. The performance of the currency options business at the NAB was monitored using this type of approach, where significant bonuses were rewarded if the revenue generated by the business was above a certain target.

Cadsby and his colleagues found that despite there being no difference in the performance between the three groups, the amount of cheating, in the form of claiming words that were not actually created, was higher for participants in group (b). This was despite the fact that, although not identical, the targets for groups (b) and (c) were very similar. What's more, the level of cheating in this group was higher when a participant's actual performance was near the specified target of nine words. This latter finding was similar to that obtained in a study conducted by Maurice Schweitzer and his colleagues,[30] and adds some weight to a thesis developed by Michael Jensen that questions the efficacy of target-based bonus schemes, suggesting that they should be replaced by linear-based compensation schemes.[31]

In summary, the research into goals clearly illustrates that when ambitious targets are used in an environment that promotes an obsessive pursuit of these goals, people show a greater preparedness to act inappropriately to hit these targets. Furthermore, adding lucrative contingent rewards into this mix just adds fuel to the fire. All these variables were in play in the period leading up to the FX trading scandal at the NAB. As mentioned earlier, there was an obsessive focus on reaching revenue targets, and there was the promise of lucrative rewards if this was achieved. Furthermore, the revenue targets grew significantly year on year, reaching levels which could easily be described as ambitious. As the business behind the scandal was offering a new product, there were expectations it would grow aggressively.

My experience has shown me how easily businesses can fall into the trap of setting ambitious performance goals. This is particularly common when a business has a track record of success, and expectations grow that future performance will continue to follow the historical trajectory. This trend, where historical outperformance leads to increased expectations and higher performance benchmarks, requires a business to grow period on period indefinitely, a path that is not sustainable. The term "Red Queen Effect" has been coined to describe this situation in competitive strategy, where a business must continue to grow and outperform period on period just to maintain its market position.[32]

It is also worth noting that some of the findings outlined above showing how the obsessive pursuit of goals can lead to unethical conduct are not just confined to the laboratory. In a study of manufacturing firms in the S&P 500, Yuri Mishina and his colleagues found that those companies that had a track record of outperformance versus their peers not only created heightened expectations for future performance, but also displayed an increased likelihood of engaging in illegal activity.[33] This finding was more pronounced for the companies in the study that were prominent and admired. Jared Harris and Philip Bromiley meanwhile conducted an investigation into a sample of 434 publically listed companies in the US that had misrepresented their financial statements between January 1997 and June 2002.[34] They found that the likelihood of financial statement misrepresentation increased markedly when the performance of the companies fell below that of their peers. A second factor that was found to be related to misrepresentation was the proportion of the CEO's compensation comprising of stock options, a good segue way into our next topic, reward.

REWARD

> *Money blinds us to our social relationships, creating a sense of self-sufficiency that discourages cooperation and mutual support.*[35]

> *Margaret Heffernan,* Willful Blindness

When designing reward and incentive schemes, organisations have typically adopted the approach dictated by the axiom of self-interest. Namely, humans are rational, profit-maximising agents that will respond positively when they are provided with increased monetary incentives.[36] Although evidence does exist showing that under some circumstances increased monetary incentives does motivate higher performance, research is beginning to show that the relationship between pay and performance is not that straightforward. Furthermore, research is also showing quite clearly that monetary incentives can cause people to engage in deceptive and unethical behaviour.

In the paragraphs that follow, I will review studies that illustrate how (a) increasing the salience of money as a reward can cause people to behave more dishonestly, (b) our neurological response to monetary rewards can cause us to make biased and potentially immoral decisions, and (c) although many people call for more transparency as a way of curtailing the potential adverse effects associated with reward schemes, transparency can at times drive perverse outcomes. The overarching theme in all of the research presented is that money has an uncanny ability of robbing us of our morality.

Environments that Promote Wealth can Magnify Unethical Behaviour

In some organisations, there is a disproportionate focus on money. Be it by making financial success central to their purpose, using performance measures that focus exclusively on financial returns or promising their employees lavish performance bonuses, these organisations create an environment that promotes and sanctifies wealth and personal profit. A recent study conducted by Francesca Gino and Lamar Pierce shows how these types of environments can have deleterious effects on our behaviour.[37]

In this study, Gino and Pierce had participants engage in an anagram task that required them to try to create 12 words from seven letters in a two-minute period (this approximately represented a 90 percentile level of performance). In all, the participants completed this exercise on eight occasions, and were rewarded $3.00 each time they created 12 or more words.

The participants were divided into two groups, a wealthy group and a poor group. The wealthy group entered a room that contained a table with approximately $7,000 of cash on it (Figure 3.2). As they entered the room, they were provided with $24 from this cash ($24 was the maximum amount they could earn across the eight anagram exercises). The poor group entered a room that contained a table with enough cash on it to provide each participant with their $24, which was distributed to them as they entered the room.

After completing the anagram tasks, the participants checked their answers, kept the money they had earned and returned any unearned money along with their answer sheet to the experimenter. Although all participants remained anonymous, the answer sheet and anagram tasks were secretly coded so the

Figure 3.2   Participants in the wealthy group completed the anagram task in a room that contained a table with approximately $7,000 cash on it

Source: Gino, F., & Pierce, L. (2009). The abundance effect: Unethical behavior in the presence of wealth. *Organizational Behavior and Human Decisions Processes, 109*(2), 142–155.

experimenters could deduce the amount of cheating. As Figure 3.3 illustrates, in both groups approximately 45 per cent of the participants actually reached the 12 word target. However, almost 78 per cent of participants claimed to have done so in the wealthy group, while 58 per cent of participants claimed to have done so in the poor group. In a subsequent experiment, Gino and Pierce found that being in the wealthy group elicited greater feelings of envy, and this is what potentially explained the increased level of unethical behaviour in that group.

Although this experiment was conducted in laboratory settings, one should not underestimate the parallels with real-life work environments. The world of financial markets and investment banking is a case in point. In some institutions, the amount paid in bonuses outstrips that paid in dividends,[38] creating environments that attract people who sanctify money and join the industry with the sole intent of becoming wealthy. In these environments, people quickly figure out who the "richest guys in the room" are, and they are lauded and placed on a pedestal, becoming the envy of those around them. The bonus period is a particularly amusing time of the year, as rumours begin circulating of who are the "winners" and "losers". The "losers", despite their gross salary still being multiples of the average wage, become disillusioned at

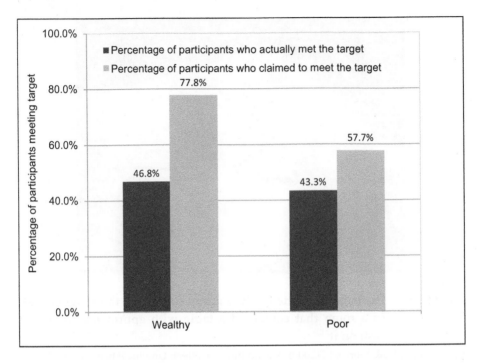

Figure 3.3   The percentage of participants who actually and claimed
                to have created 12 words in the anagram task. The wealthy
                group completed the anagram task in a room containing a
                table with approximately $7,000 cash on it, while the room in
                which the poor group completed the task in contained a table
                with sufficient cash on it to cover the maximum reward the
                participants could potentially earn from their involvement in
                the study

Source: Gino, F., & Pierce, L. (2009). The abundance effect: Unethical behavior in the
presence of wealth. *Organizational Behavior and Human Decisions Processes, 109(2),*
142–155.

the perceived inequality, a response that although bemusing is not surprising
given how people display a preference for higher relative rather than absolute
income levels.[39] It is little wonder that these types of environments are so often
the crucible for immoral behaviour.

The Neuroscience of Monetary Rewards

As we have already seen, the field of neuroscience has enabled us to identify
some of the neurological underpinnings of human behaviour. Our response
to monetary rewards has also been the subject of research in this field, with

studies showing that the mere anticipation of a monetary payment results in the reward regions of the brain becoming active.[40]

More recent research has also illustrated how our neurological response to reward can drive biased and potentially unethical decision making. Ann Harvey and her colleagues conducted a study where participants were told that the payment they would receive for being involved was to be provided by one of two companies.[41] Their task was to evaluate artwork from these two companies. While sitting in a brain-imaging machine, the participants viewed a series of 60 paintings, each one paired with either the logo of the sponsoring company or the logo of the non-sponsoring company. After completing this part of the study, the participants viewed all of the paintings again with the company logos, this time assigning a rating to them.

As expected, the ratings assigned by the participants displayed a distinct preference for the paintings that were associated with their sponsoring company, especially when the amount they were paid by the sponsoring company increased (participants received either $30, $100 or $300). What was more revealing, however, were the results from the neuroimaging task. These suggested there was a neurological basis for the participants' preferences, as the regions of the brain associated with preference and pleasure were more active when participants viewed paintings containing the logo of their sponsoring company. Furthermore, the level of activation in these regions was more elevated as the level of payment to the participants increased. Results like these provide one explanation for why in the lead-up to the global financial crisis, credit-rating agencies provided investment-grade ratings for securities underpinned by subprime mortgages – they were being paid handsomely by the institutions issuing the securities for their "independent" opinion.

As Harvey and her colleagues pointed out, there are obvious parallels between their findings and those of James Rilling and his colleagues that found a neurological basis for reciprocation of cooperative responses in the Prisoner's Dilemma Game. As humans, we feel a sense of indebtedness to those who do us a favour, and this has neurological underpinnings. Although this can drive reciprocity and cooperation, as the study by Harvey and her colleagues shows, it can also drive biased (and potentially unethical) judgment. One can easily see how in a workplace, if someone is being handsomely rewarded by their superiors for engaging in conduct that could be deemed unethical, then the reward would only serve to condone and further encourage this behaviour, especially if it is undertaken with their superior's knowledge.

Transparency Might be Necessary, but it is Definitely not Sufficient

The study by Harvey and her colleagues is a classic illustration of a conflict of interest. Conflicts of interest arise when an individual's personal interest is at odds with their professional responsibilities. In the experiment above, the participants' personal interest (looking after the company that paid for their attendance) conflicted with their responsibility (providing unbiased ratings for the quality of the artwork). Conflicts of interest are endemic in the business world, as many people are typically rewarded on their ability to sell a product or service. What's more, there is more often than not information asymmetry between the individual providing the product or service and the end purchaser.

The general response to conflicts of interest has typically involved increased disclosure and transparency. On the face of it, this approach would appear to rectify the potential for any immoral or unjust outcomes. Armed with this knowledge, the buyer would be able to appropriately discount any information or advice they receive from the conflicted party and make better decisions. However, recent research has shown that disclosure and transparency can have perverse outcomes. A clever study undertaken by Daylian Cain and his colleagues is a perfect illustration of this.[42]

In this study, participants were randomly assigned to play the role of "estimator" or "advisor". As the labels suggest, estimators were required to estimate an uncertain quantity, namely the amount of money in a jar full of coins. Advisors meanwhile provided advice to the estimators to assist them in making their predictions. Advisors were given the opportunity to observe the jar for an extended period of time and were informed that the amount of money in the jars ranged from $10 to $20. This provided them with superior information relative to the estimator, establishing information asymmetry. There was a total of six rounds, and in each round the amount of money in the jar varied.

Cain and his colleagues ran three scenarios. In the first, both advisors and estimators were paid according to the accuracy of the estimator's predictions. Both estimators and advisors in this scenario were aware that their incentives were aligned. In the second scenario, advisors were remunerated more when the predictions of the estimators were higher than the actual amount of money in the jar. Estimators meanwhile were always paid according to the accuracy of their predictions. The advisor's conflict of interest was not disclosed to the estimator in this scenario. The third and final scenario was identical to the second, except that the advisor's conflict of interest was known to the estimator.

In addition to these rewards, advisors were provided with another opportunity to earn money by providing their own personal best prediction of the amount of money in the jars.

The results, illustrated in Figure 3.4, reveal an interesting pattern. Firstly, and as expected, the advisors' suggestion to the estimator increased between scenarios one and two. That is, as the advisors' interest shifted from having the estimator provide accurate predictions to providing higher predictions, their suggestions also increased in value. Surprisingly, however, there was a further increase in the advisors' suggestion between scenarios two and three. Recall that

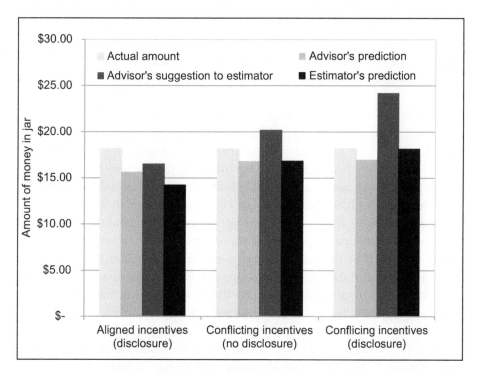

Figure 3.4   Amount of money in the jars (displayed as averages). For each of the three scenarios, the results display the following outcomes: (a) the actual amount of money in the jar, (b) the amount the advisor predicted was in the jar, (c) the amount the advisor suggested to the estimator was in the jar, and (d) the amount the estimator predicted was in the jar after learning of the advisor's suggestion

Source: Cain, D. M., Loewenstein, G., & Moore, D. A. (2005). The dirt on coming clean: Perverse effects of disclosing conflicts of interest. *Journal of Legal Studies, 34*(1), 1–25. University of Chicago Press.

the nature of the advisors' conflict did not change between these scenarios – all that changed was the disclosure of conflict. As Cain and his colleagues propose, it is as if disclosure provided the advisors with a "moral license", reducing any feelings of guilt associated with providing biased advice and misleading the estimators. One could easily foresee a situation where, if transparency allowed this type of conduct to continue unabated, it would risk becoming normalised.

The results also show that in the two conflict of interest scenarios, the estimator did discount the suggested value provided by the advisor. However, although the level of discounting was greater in the scenario where the conflict of interest was disclosed, it was not sufficient to offset the inflated value provided by the advisor in this scenario. This perverse outcome associated with disclosure was validated by the final payments to participants, which showed that advisors earned more money in the scenario when their conflict of interest was disclosed, and estimators made the least money in this scenario.

So what are we to make of all of the above research? Clearly, money has the ability to significantly compromise our morality. Organisations where money, wealth and financial success are sanctified and play a central role in their reason for being create an environment that is fertile for unethical conduct. The above results are arguably best summarised by a series of studies undertaken by Kathleen Vohs and her colleagues, which showed how even subtle reminders of money can cause people to take on a more self-centred orientation.[43] Participants primed to think about money were less likely to render assistance or donate to a charity, displayed a greater desire to work and play alone, and were more protective of their personal space. If empathy, cooperation, reciprocity and altruism are the pillars of ethics, then money is not a mechanism that will lay the foundations for ethical conduct.

However, a focus on money is not just detrimental for the ethics of an organisation. Research is also showing that money is only effective as a motivator for specific tasks. In his book *Drive*,[44] Daniel Pink popularised research undertaken by Dan Ariely and his colleagues that illustrated how monetary incentives appear only to be effective in inducing increased performance for tasks that are repetitive and mundane in nature.[45] As the authors concluded in their paper:

> *Tasks that involve only effort are likely to benefit from increased incentives, while for tasks that include a cognitive component, there seems to be a level of incentive beyond which further increases can have detrimental effects on performance.*

The idea that monetary incentives stifle creativity is not new. In a study conducted in 1962, Sam Glucksberg employed the so-called "candle problem" to illustrate how rewards can hamper creative thought.[46] Fist devised by Karl Duncker, the candle problem provides participants with a box of matches, a box of thumbtacks and a candle, and asks them to mount the candle to a wall.[47] In his original study, Duncker found that a large determinant of a participant's success in solving the problem was whether the thumbtacks were provided to them within or outside of the box. When the thumbtacks were within the box, participants displayed "functional fixedness" – they were less likely to think creatively and see that in addition to being a storage device for the thumbtacks, the box could also, by using the thumbtacks, be mounted to the wall and act as a platform for the candle. When repeating the study years later, Glucksberg found that the tendency towards functional fixedness was more pronounced when participants were provided with a monetary incentive to solve the problem.

The majority of senior leader roles demand a large degree of higher-order cognitive thinking, as the problems people in these roles are required to solve, and the decisions they are called on to make, are more often than not shrouded with a high degree of complexity and ambiguity. One could quite easily mount an argument that current executive pay structures fail to promote the type of creative thinking that senior executive roles demand. Furthermore, correlational studies are consistently showing that there is negligible relationship between the pay level of the most senior executives and the performance of the organisations they manage.[48] Redressing executive remuneration practices is not just an exercise organisations should embark on because of its symbolism – it also makes a lot of sense.

So what is the solution? Like all the issues addressed in this book, there is no silver bullet. Furthermore, I don't think the answer lies solely in the design of performance and reward frameworks. No performance and reward framework is perfect, albeit some are better than others. However, a good starting point would be to recognise that the model of human behaviour that has been used to guide the design of performance and reward frameworks, namely the axiom of self-interest, has significant shortcomings.

As a first step, leaders must strive to articulate a meaningful social purpose for their organisations that is underpinned by a virtuous set of values. A venal purpose that focuses on profit, self-promotion, competition or market share will act as a lure to unethical conduct. Alternatively, by connecting employees to a virtuous purpose, it is possible for an organisation to cultivate a relationship with its people that is more social in nature rather than commercial, thus tapping into their capacity and desire for connection, cooperation and reciprocity.

James Heyman and Dan Ariely cleverly illustrated that two types of markets exists for the provision of human effort, namely a "social" market and a "monetary" market.[49] Using repetitive, mundane tasks, Heyman and Ariely showed that in social markets where participants were awarded with a gift (candy), the level of effort provided remained constant regardless of how much candy was offered. In monetary markets, the level of effort increased when monetary payment increased, and only reached the level of the social market when monetary payment was high. This led them to draw the following conclusion:

> When payments were given in the form of gifts (candy) or when payments were not mentioned, effort seemed to stem from altruistic motives and was largely insensitive to the magnitude of the payment. In contrast, when payments were given in the form of cash, effort seemed to stem from reciprocation motives and was sensitive to the magnitude of the payment.

Meanwhile, in research conducted outside the laboratory, it has been illustrated how switching an agreement from one that is commercial to one that is social in nature (or vice versa) can alter an individual's motivation and "moral" commitment. For example, Carl Mellström and Magnus Johannesson conducted a study in Sweden that showed that only 30 per cent of female participants agreed to become blood donors when a monetary payment was offered, compared to 52 per cent when no such payment was offered.[50] Interestingly, 53 per cent of participants agreed to become blood donors when there was the option to donate the monetary payment to a charity. Uri Gneezy and Aldo Rustichini showed that when a monetary fine was imposed on parents who failed to collect their children on time from child care centres in the town of Haifa in Israel, the level of delinquency actually increased.[51] Meanwhile, Adam Grant and his colleagues found that when employees in the call centre of a fundraising organisation had the opportunity to engage and interact with the beneficiaries of the donations they procured (undergraduate student scholarship recipients), the amount of time they spent on the phone and the amount of money they raised increased by 142 per cent and 171 per cent respectively.[52]

The banking and finance industry is arguably the canonical example of what can occur when institutions slowly but insidiously decrease their focus on the communities they serve in favour of an increased focus on money, wealth and personal profit. There was a time when banking was a reputable and honourable profession. The industry was deeply connected to the clients they served and bankers were held in high regard by the community. Bankers did not abuse this status, but rather accepted it with humility, never losing sight of their responsibility to their clients and communities.

Over time, this ethos eroded and has been replaced by a self-centered orientation. Instead of joining the industry to serve the community, many people join to make money, get rich and serve themselves to the detriment of others (so-called "rent-seeking" behaviour). In a recent speech delivered by the Governor of the Bank of England, Mark Carney, he spoke about the issues associated with this type of orientation and how it played a pivotal role in the global financial crisis:[53]

> *In the run-up to the crisis, banking became about banks not businesses; transactions not relations; counterparties not clients. New instruments originally designed to meet the credit and hedging needs of businesses quickly morphed into ways to amplify bets on financial outcomes.*

> *When bankers become detached from end-users, their only reward becomes money. Purely financial compensation ignores the non-pecuniary rewards to employment, such as the satisfaction from helping a client or colleague succeed.*

Thus, as outlined above, the challenge facing all organisations, especially the institutions within the banking and finance industry, is to create a virtuous social purpose that connects employees to the communities they serve, and places service to others and a higher purpose ahead of service to self. As Mark Carney went on to articulate in the same speech, this all begins with leadership:

> *This process begins with boards and senior management defining clearly the purpose of their organisations and promoting a culture of ethical business throughout them. Employees must be grounded in strong connections to their clients and their communities. To move to a world that once again values the future, bankers need to see themselves as custodians of their institutions, improving them before passing them along to their successors.*

Power

> *Your faith was strong but you needed proof*
> *You saw her bathing on the roof*
> *Her beauty in the moonlight overthrew you.*[54]

Leonard Cohen, "Hallelujah"

Given that the majority of modern organisations are structured around a status hierarchy, power is a ubiquitous force within them. In chapter one, we showed how people in positions of power within an organisation have a disproportionate impact in shaping context, and how this context can foster and promote unethical behaviour. Through their actions, choices and decisions, senior leaders send powerful messages to their people about the type of conduct that is acceptable and, more importantly, the type of conduct that will be rewarded and get you ahead. In chapter two, we discussed how power operates in groups, and how those in positions of authority can elicit obedience and cause people to behave in ways they would consider to be totally inappropriate when acting alone. In this section, we discuss how the psychological experience of power can corrupt and debase our moral character.

Literature of all genres is replete with stories and tales of how power has corrupted individuals and caused them to behave in unethical and at times criminal ways. One such story is that of King David, which appears in both the Old Testament and the Torah, and receives mention in Leonard Cohen's famous song "Hallelujah". From all accounts, David was a man of high moral character who came from humble beginnings. His strategic vision, intelligence, charisma and courage on the field of battle saw him have a meteoric rise to power. He was a leader with extraordinary influence, wealth and popularity. Yet when he was at the top of his game, he entered into an adulterous affair with Bathsheba while her husband Uriah was fighting in David's army. Following his indulgence, David's moral conduct degenerated as he attempted to cover up his wrongdoing, and this eventually led him to arrange for Uriah to be sent to his death in the field of battle.

This storyline is not unfamiliar. So often we see leaders at the top of their game succumb to the trappings of office. Greed and hubris takeover, and this leads to immoral and at times unlawful behaviour. As Joseph Badaracco puts it, these leaders seem to be unable to "resist the flow of success".[55] An element of this pattern of behaviour underlies all of the well known ethical failures in the business world, and the FX trading incident at the NAB was no exception.

People in positions of power, some without realising it, exploit their authority and privileged control of resources and people to not only engage in and cover up unethical behaviour, but also seduce other people to join them in the journey.

The story of King David led Dean Ludwig and Clinton Longenecker to label this phenomenon "the Bathsheba Syndrome".[56] According to Ludwig and Longenecker, success is an antecedent of ethical failure, and contains "the very seeds that could lead to the downfall of both the leader and the organization". Specifically, they call out four byproducts of success that can lead to ethical failure, namely complacency and a loss of strategic focus, privileged access to both information and people, increasing control over resources, and an inflated belief in one's ability to manipulate and control outcomes. With these dynamics at play, Ludwig and Longenecker argue that even the most moral person can be seduced into behaving in unethical ways.

THE CORRUPTING INFLUENCE OF POWER

In more recent times, the field of psychology has attempted to provide more scientific rigour to the study of power, and has investigated this notion that the experience of power corrupts by having metamorphic effects on a person's psychological processes. Research of this genre has involved making some of the participants in the studies feel more powerful by either (a) providing them with control over resources or other people in the study, or (b) priming them to feel more powerful (typically done by asking them to recall and write about a personally meaningful experience where they possessed power). This research has provided some revealing insights into how the psychological experience of power can effect behaviour.

To begin with, many of the findings provide clear support for the notion that power corrupts. In one of the pioneering studies, David Kipnis had participants manage "workers" located in a separate room who were producing a good.[57] Some of the participants were provided with a range of institutional powers, including the ability to control reward and replace or fire workers. Kipnis found that compared to participants who were not provided with these institutional powers, powerful participants showed a greater propensity to view workers as objects to be manipulated, valued the output of the workers less, and were less willing to interact with the workers socially.

In a more recent study conducted by Samuel Bendahan and his colleagues, participants took part in a social dilemma game where the appointed leader had to divide a sum of money between themselves and other participants they were paired with.[58] The leaders were provided with the following three allocation options: (a) "Default", where the leader received slightly more than the participants, (b) "Prosocial", where the money was evenly split, and (c) "Antisocial", where the leader received even more than what was proposed in the default option, to the detriment of the other participants. The power of the leader in the study was manipulated using two methods. Firstly, some of the leaders were placed in larger groups thus requiring them to make the distribution decision for more people (leaders were placed in charge of either one or three other participants). Secondly, some leaders were provided with a fourth allocation option, which skewed the distribution of the funds even further in the favour of the leader than the antisocial option.

Prior to commencing the social dilemma game, the participants were asked how a "responsible leader" would allocate the funds. This exercise enabled the researchers to establish a social norm. Just under 81 per cent of the participants endorsed the default option, while 16 per cent endorsed the prosocial option (only 3.3 per cent endorsed the antisocial option). The response from the participants who were subsequently nominated to be leaders in the study did not differ dramatically from this distribution (82 per cent, 14 per cent and 4 per cent respectively). Furthermore, the participants also completed personality tests to allow the researchers to determine if differences in the leader's level of honesty was driving distribution decisions, rather than power.

Despite being aware of the prevailing social norms, leaders in the low-power groups chose the antisocial allocation option just over 53 per cent of the time, a marked departure from the social norm. Leaders in the high power groups meanwhile chose the antisocial option over 80 per cent of the time, showing complete disregard for the social norm. In addition, the researchers found that the leader's honesty did not play a role in explaining their allocation decisions. The conclusion provided by the researchers was straightforward – power corrupts:

> ... *as our results show, even those who were honest and had mostly socially-acceptable attitudes at the moment of their accession to a position of leadership rather easily changed their moral perspectives once they got a taste of power.*

Although the above research supports the notion that the psychological experience of power can corrupt, there have also been some contradictory findings. As the next section illustrates, researchers have also shown that in some cases, power is not necessarily a force for evil.

THE DIVERGENT EFFECTS OF POWER

Without going through all the research in this area (as it is voluminous), a clever study conducted by Adam Galinsky and his colleagues eloquently illustrates some of the seemingly dichotomous findings.[59] The study made use of two different types of social dilemmas, namely the commons dilemma and the public goods dilemma. These two social dilemmas have some parallels with the Prisoner's Dilemma Game, as they call for participants to choose between behaving in a cooperative or a self-interested manner. In the commons dilemma, participants decide how much of a shared resource they take for themselves. Showing restraint will mean that the shared resource will survive while still allowing for consumption in the short term. It is analogous to the dilemma faced by commercial fishing operations. In the public goods dilemma, participants must decide how much to contribute to create a shared resource. Failure to contribute not only places the survival of the shared resource at risk, but also means there is freeloading. It is analogous to the dilemma one faces when deciding whether they should contribute to a community radio station.

Although both these social dilemmas involve a trade-off between having more for oneself versus acting in the interest of the collective, they are psychologically very different. One is a decision around consumption (commons dilemma), while the other is a decision around contribution (public goods dilemma).

Galinsky and his colleagues structured the study in such a way that in the commons dilemma, there was a pool of 1,000 points. During each round, participants could take between zero to ten points for themselves. The aim was to accumulate as many points as possible for yourself, as the personal tally would determine how many lottery tickets the participants would receive at the end of the study. However, if after two rounds there is nothing remaining in the common pool, then no lottery tickets would be issued. In the public goods dilemma, participants were told that the opening balance of the common pool was negative 1,000 points, and that the aim was to make the balance positive over two rounds. At the beginning of each round, participants were credited with ten points, and they would need to decide how many of these to contribute to the common pool. Once again, the aim was to accumulate as many points as possible for yourself in order to earn lottery tickets; however, no lottery tickets would be distributed if the balance in the common pool was below zero after two rounds.

The results were insightful. In the commons dilemma, relative to low-power participants, high-power participants displayed greater self-interest and took more from the common pool of resources. Furthermore, the resource pool was depleted after two rounds, but would have survived beyond the second round if the study was carried out using only low-power participants. In the public goods dilemma meanwhile, high power participants displayed greater cooperation relative to low-power participants, and contributed more to the common pool of resources. Like the commons dilemma, the resource pool failed to survive beyond the second round. However, unlike the commons dilemma, survival of the resource pool would have been assured if the study was carried out using only high power participants. As Galinsky and his colleagues state:

> *Power is linked to the depletion of a valued resource in one case and the continuation of a valued resource in the other case. A community of high-power individuals could be a condemned community suffering deprivation or a confident community reveling in an ever-expanding public resource.*

How does one explain this seemingly contradictory influence on behaviour created by power? Does power always corrupt as much as the literature suggests, or are there times when it can act as a force for good? A theory has been developed that goes some way to explaining these divergent findings and other similar results. The "approach/inhibition theory" of power[60] proposes that power activates approach tendencies. Among other things, it suggests that those in possession of power tend to be less inhibited, display a tendency towards action, exhibit goal-directed behaviour and focus on rewards. The powerless meanwhile are more inhibited, display heightened vigilance towards possible threats and punishments in the environment, and behave in ways that place the interests of others ahead of themselves. According to the theory, the approach tendencies elicited by power can at times motivate behaviour that is ethical and prosocial.

For example, this model can explain the seemingly contradictory findings in the study conducted by Galinsky and his colleagues, as the experience of power increases the tendency towards taking action. For the commons dilemma, taking action results in antisocial behaviour as the powerful participants took more from the common resource pool to the detriment of other participants. For the public goods dilemma though, taking action means contributing to the common resource pool to the detriment of one's own interests. As Galinsky and his colleagues describe, the dichotomous outcomes that the action orientation of the powerful creates can also significantly alter how we perceive the powerful:[61]

> *In a commons dilemma, those experiencing power would appear to perpetuate power's reputation as a scourge and blight, exhibiting greater antisocial tendencies than those with less power. In a public goods dilemma, however, those experiencing power would resemble admired public figures who create prosocial outcomes that would otherwise not materialize.*

THE MODERATING EFFECT OF GOALS

From a practitioner's perspective, it is important to get a sense for the types of circumstances that can cause power to corrupt, and the circumstances in which it can act as a force for good and promote allocentric, ethical outcomes. This is particularly important in light of recent research by Marko Pitesa and Stefan Thau, which showed how power increases focus on oneself, making the powerful less likely to be influenced by context and social norms.[62] This finding is at complete odds with some of the research that has been discussed in the previous two chapters of this book, and suggests that even in organisations that foster and promote ethical behaviour, the self-focus of those in positions of power can mean they follow their own preferences, regardless of whether they are aligned to the prevailing norms.

Like Pitesa and Thau, an earlier study by Adam Galinsky and his colleagues also found that powerful people were less influenced by the situation.[63] To explain their results, Galinsky and his colleagues pointed to the pivotal role of goals and drew the following conclusion:

> *How do we reconcile our findings that power reduces the strength of the situation with research showing that the powerful are sometimes more responsive to the situation than the powerless? We think the key moderating variable is goals. One of the most robust findings emerging from the literature on power is that power increases goal-directed behaviour and cognition.*

As the approach/inhibition theory proposes, power promotes goal pursuit. Powerful people show greater goal-directed actions. They are more resilient in the face of obstacles, are more likely to seize opportunities that facilitate goal pursuit, and focus attention on goal-relevant information while ignoring distracting information. Research undertaken by Ana Guinote led her to conclude that powerful people tend to operate in an "if–then" fashion, conditioning their response depending on the situation.[64] In her study, Guinote showed that when high-power participants were provided with a goal, they responded selectively to the situation, prioritising information that facilitated goal pursuit.

These findings build on and reinforce the conclusions drawn in previous sections of this chapter. An obsessive focus on ambitious goals that are linked to high monetary stakes is a dangerous mix. Adding power to this mix makes it toxic. The importance of articulating a virtuous purpose and connecting people in the organisation (especially the powerful) to it, cannot be underestimated. When leaders foster environments that value financial performance, wealth, personal profit, promotion and a "win at all cost" attitude, then like moths to a bright light, the powerful within the organisation will instinctively behave in a way that will allow these values to flourish.

This was eloquently illustrated in a study conducted by Jennifer Overbeck and Bernadette Park, where participants were assigned to the role of senior managers in one of two companies.[65] The first company had a proud history of putting its people first, something that was emphasised by the wording of its mission statement that demonstrated "people-orientated" values. The second company valued financial outcomes and efficiency, and this was once again emphasised in the mission statement that highlighted the priority placed on optimal production, profit maximisation, and "production-orientated" values.

Participants were then asked to complete two tasks. The first was to write a "state of the company" report, which was to be presented to the board of directors. The second involved ranking 20 items of current importance to the company, ten of which were people-related issues, and ten of which were financial-related issues. The participants who worked as senior managers in the company with "people-orientated" values incorporated more information about people-related issues in the "state of the company" report, and included more people-related items in their top five rankings of issues currently important to the company. For the participants working as senior managers in the company with "production-orientated" values meanwhile, the results followed the opposite trend, with far greater emphasis being placed on financial-related issues in both the "state of the company" report and in the top five rankings of issues. As Overbeck and Park state:

People assigned to powerful roles in a workgroup were more responsive to the stated values and goals of the organization that empowered them: They used value-consistent information more in their reports on the state of the organization, and they ranked such information as more important to the continued functioning of the company.

As mentioned earlier, power is ubiquitous in all organisations, and will continue to be so as long as the structure of organisations is based on a status hierarchy. So, while we may not be able to control the tendency for powerful people to respond in an action-orientated and goal-directed manner, we can ensure that we develop a virtuous purpose for our organisations, and develop ways to meaningfully engage people in positions of power with this purpose. As Deborah Gruenfeld and her colleagues state:[66]

We often assume that power inherently activates self-serving goals in the power holder, but in some studies, this assumption is not borne out. Perhaps the issue is finding ways to engage power holders more fully in the meaning and responsibilities associated with their organizational roles, as opposed to concerns with self-promotion, self-protection, or self-enhancement.

Fear

When we do not understand death, we do not understand life.[67]

Sogyal Rinpoche

Both during my time in financial markets and subsequent experience in the corporate world, it has become clear to me that there is a driver of behaviour within organisations that goes beyond money and power. People within organisations, especially the most senior and powerful, have worked for years to attain a status or title that they become highly attached to, is central to their identity, and defines who they are. When their position is threatened, be it due to poor performance, feelings of incompetence, changes in organisational structure or the risk of having previous maleficence uncovered, the natural response is to go to extreme lengths to defend and protect this position. What is driving this defensive response is the fear associated with the loss of their status and title, and the associated financial rewards and lifestyle the position affords. By extension, what is at stake is their very sense of self and identity.

The previous section showed how the psychological experience of power can have deleterious effects on the powerful as they pursue self-enhancement and success. However, research has also shown that when the position of a powerful individual is under threat, this can also lead to conduct that is consistent with the view that power corrupts. In a series of studies, Nathanael Fast and Serena Chen showed that when a person in a position of power felt incompetent, they were more likely to exhibit aggressive behaviour.[68] However, this aggressiveness was eliminated when the participant's sense of self-worth was boosted, leading the authors to conclude:

> Taken together these findings suggest that (a) power paired with self-perceived incompetence leads to aggression, and (b) this aggressive response is driven by feelings of ego defensiveness.

THE CENTRAL ROLE OF SELF-ESTEEM

Psychologists will admit that it is difficult to find a definitive and coherent definition for concepts like "ego" and "ego defensiveness". However, generally speaking, when psychologists talk about ego threat, they are more often than not referring to threats to our self-esteem.[69] Broadly defined, self-esteem refers to how we evaluate our own worth. A finding that has unanimous support in the field of psychology is that, as humans, we have an insatiable desire to enhance and protect our self-esteem. What's more, research has found that we have developed some ingenious ways of meeting this goal:

- We develop causal explanations for social outcomes in such a way that we attribute positive outcomes to ourselves and negative outcomes to others or circumstance (the so-called self-serving bias).[70]

- We display biased memory, seeming to be more adept at recalling our successes and positive attributes while forgetting our failures and negative attributes (so-called mnemic neglect).[71]

- We engage in strategic social comparisons, showing a preference for comparing ourselves against people we consider to be inferior to us (i.e. "downward comparisons").[72]

- We consider ourselves to be above average on a variety of personality traits, especially for traits that are considered to be most desirable (the so-called better than average effect).[73]

- We subtly shift how we define concepts like virtue and talent in such a way that our definitions are aligned with attributes we possess, while our definitions for concepts like vice and deficiency favours attributes we lack (so-called strategic construal).[74]

- We expend psychological resources refuting information that threatens our self-esteem, adopting a critical attitude towards blame and a favourable attitude towards praise.[75]

- We overestimate our abilities in an array of social and intellectual domains, and this propensity tends to increase the more incompetent we are (the so-called Dunning–Kruger effect).[76]

- There are neurological underpinnings for our desire to enhance and protect our self-esteem, with neuroscientists showing that acquiring a good reputation activates the same reward centres of the brain that are activated when we receive a monetary reward.[77]

In addition to the above, self-esteem is one of the primary reasons why we put so much effort into curating our identities – we are highly motivated to develop a self-concept that makes us feel good about ourselves.[78] Whenever our identity and self-concept are threatened, we become fearful and anxious, because ultimately what is at stake is our self-esteem. So often we see a leader's identity defined by the positions of power they occupy, and when their hold on these positions becomes tenuous, the associated anxiety and fear drives defensive behaviours that can often cross the line and become unethical.

When given the choice between being humble or being egotistical, we have a strong predilection for the latter, a choice that so often ends in humility when our self-esteem is threatened. We spend our lives building our self-esteem and erecting large barriers to defend it. The narcissist, a personality type that is more likely to emerge in senior leadershp ranks, is particularly adroit at doing this.[79] When those barriers begin to crumble, the consequences associated with the personal response that follows can be disastrous, and for leaders, these consequences can extend to the organisations and the communities they serve.

There is now ample research illustrating how situations that threaten our self-esteem can elicit undesirable and unethical behaviour. In recent research conducted by Celia Moore and her colleagues, it was shown that when a participants' competence (a key diver of self-esteem) was challenged, they displayed a greater preparedness to engage in dishonest behaviour.[80] In a series of studies, Moore and her colleagues randomly assigned participants to two groups. One group was made to believe that the task they were completing was easy, while the other group was made to believe it was hard. When the participants were provided with the opportunity to cheat, those who were told the task was easy, and therefore had higher performance expectations, were more likely to avail themselves of this opportunity. According to the authors, performing below expectations would have compromised their view of their own competence, and in order to resolve the resulting dissonance they behaved dishonestly.

Meanwhile, John Georgesen and Monica Harris conducted a study in which a participant's self-esteem was threatened by making them feel that their position of power and leadership was potentially terminal.[81] In their study, Georgesen and Harris had participants work in groups of two to work on a problem-solving task. One of the participants was chosen to be the leader and assigned duties that are typically associated with positions of power (such as evaluating performance and determining reward). For some of the dyads, the leader was made to feel that their position was under threat and that they would be required to swap positions with their partner if they did not perform. Among other things, Georgesen and Harris found that when the participant chosen to be leader felt that their position was unstable, they attempted to exert more control in their interaction with their partner, felt more threatened when they were informed that their partner was very capable, and asserted more strongly that they deserved to be the boss. Once again, these are responses that are typical of someone trying to protect their status and self-esteem.

Perhaps more fascinating are theories that have been put forward to try to provide answers to some of the deeper questions that flow from these types of findings: Why do we place such a huge premium on our self-esteem? Why do we expend so much effort building our self-esteem, and go to such extreme lengths to defend it when it is threatened? Among the theories that have been proposed, one that has received considerable currency in recent times is terror management theory. It suggests that our deep desire to build and protect our self-esteem is rooted in a uniquely human attribute that is central to the human condition – the awareness of our mortality.

TERROR MANAGEMENT THEORY

Writings on the central role of death and the awareness of our mortality plays in the lives of humans can be traced as far back to 3,000 BCE.[82] These writings highlight the unique dilemma we face as humans. To begin with, our cognitive abilities have evolved in such a way that we are self-aware, and can think in terms of the past, the present and the future. This allows us to not only create an identity for ourselves that aligns with our narrative of the past, but also to make plans for ourselves in the future. Conversely, our cognitive abilities also make us acutely aware of our own mortality. Herein lies the dilemma. At some point in time, the identity we have strived to create for ourselves ceases to exist. Our identity, and all the symbolisms associated with it (our material possessions, titles, biography, etc.) are essentially impermanent. As Sogyal Rinpoche puts it so eloquently:[83]

> *Perhaps the deepest reason why we are afraid of death is because we do not know who we are. We believe in a personal, unique, and separate identity — but if we dare to examine it, we find that this identity depends entirely on an endless collection of things to prop it up: Our name, our "biography," our partners, family, home, job, friends, credit cards ... It is on their fragile and transient support that we rely for our security. So when they are all taken away, will we have any idea of who we really are?*

First proposed in 1986 by Jeff Greenberg, Tom Pyszczynski and Sheldon Solomon, the basis for terror management theory (TMT) is this unique existential dilemma faced by humans – we hold a deep desire for life and a future, yet are acutely aware that it is finite. The theory proposes that the awareness of our inevitable death creates paralysing fear or terror, and we address this by employing defence mechanisms. Although largely attributed to Freud, the concept of defence mechanisms can be traced back to the writings of Danish philosopher Søren Kierkegaard.[84] In TMT, the key defence mechanism employed to protect against the terror associated with our knowledge of our mortality is self-esteem. As Tom Pyszczynski and his colleagues explain:[85]

> *The crux of the terror management answer to the question, Why do people need self-esteem? is that self-esteem functions to shelter people from deeply rooted anxiety inherent in the human condition. Self-esteem is a protective shield designed to control the potential for terror that results from awareness of the horrifying possibility that we humans are merely transient animals groping to survive in a meaningless universe, destined only to die and decay. From this perspective, then, each individual human's name and identity, family and social identifications, goals and aspirations, occupation and title, are humanly created adornments draped over an animal that, in the cosmic scheme*

of things, may be no more significant or enduring than any individual potato, pineapple, or porcupine. But it is this elaborate drapery that provides us with the fortitude to carry on despite the uniquely human awareness of our mortal fate.

There is now a growing body of literature providing support for TMT. Of the various ways the theory is tested, a common methodology employed involves investigating whether making people aware of their mortality (so-called "mortality salience") induces behaviour that enhances self-esteem. Countless studies have shown this to be the case. It is important to note that because people derive self-esteem from different sources, there are individual differences in how people respond to mortality salience. As an example, in Western cultures where individualism, materialism and financial success are highly valued, mortality salience increases the appeal of high-status items.[86] In collectivist cultures like Japan, where materialism is not as highly valued, people do not respond in the same way to mortality salience, but still engage in behaviours that seek to bolster self-esteem.[87]

With respect to business ethics, TMT provides a plausible explanation for much of the unethical behaviour we witness in the corporate world. Generally speaking, senior leaders place a premium on the power, status and the prestige associated with their roles – it becomes a core component of their identity and how they define themselves. When poor performance, feelings of incompetence, restructures or other events create the perception that their positions are terminal, fear and defensive behaviour is a typical response. This is not surprising given what is at stake – power, status, prestige – and more telling their very sense of self, their identity, and their self-esteem. It is when this response decays into ethical lapses that the consequences can be so destructive – performance levels are artificially inflated, people are misled, and past misdemeanours are covered up.

It is a pattern of behaviour that was beautifully illustrated in the film *Arbitrage*, in which Robert Miller, played by Richard Gere, was the archetype of a modern-day King David – a wealthy, highly regarded and successful hedge fund manager who seemingly had it all. The movie tracks the incredible lengths Miller went to in order to defend his status and identity: fraudulently misrepresenting the true value of his business ahead of a potential sale, covering up his involvement in a car accident that resulted in the death of a woman he was having an adulterous affair with and bribing a young man to act as his alibi. At the end of the movie, Miller's daughter, despite having knowledge of his financial fraud, provided him with a glowing introduction at a charity event for which he was a major donor. Despite his immoral conduct, Miller stood on stage, proudly accepting the rapturous applause from his adoring fans. In the end, what mattered most to Miller was that the identity he had worked so hard to create for himself, that of a successful, powerful and philanthropic professional, remained intact.

Lessons for Leaders

The unexamined life is not worth living for a human being.

Socrates, The Apology

In many ways, this is the most important chapter of the book. When a leader is not aware that money and power is seducing them to behave in ways that compromise their own or the organisation's core values, or when fear is driving defensive behaviour that is doing the same, they begin shaping environments and creating group dynamics that potentially foster unethical behaviour. A leader must develop a level of self-awareness that ensures they are vigilant to the trappings of money and power, and can appropriately deal with situations when their identity and ego is threatened. When a leader is averse to devoting the time and effort required to undertake the deep introspection to cultivate this self-awareness, they risk allowing attachments to money, power and status bring the darker sides of their character to the surface.

A simple anecdote may help to illustrate what I mean by undertaking the necessary introspection to "know thyself". In a change programme I was involved in, we asked leaders across the business to complete a leadership bio that included a leadership philosophy. In articulating their philosophy, some leaders proudly stated that they were "values based", a very interesting claim given they did not go on to articulate their values. At a subsequent event, where we brought the leaders together and shared their bios with them, one of the "values-based" leaders approached me to let me know that their business title at the top of the bio was incorrect and that this error misrepresented their standing in the organisation. From this exchange, it became clear to me that although this leader may have been "values based", what they valued was status and identity.

This is not to suggest that there is anything wrong with valuing status and identity per se. As mentioned at the beginning of this chapter, power, used correctly, can build and bind and help the organisation move towards fulfilling its purpose. However, I dare say that in claiming to be "values based", this leader would have thought their values were aligned to the virtuous values of the organisation. If they had undertaken the necessary introspection required to identify their fundamental values, they would have recognised that this was not the case. Several questions flow from this realisation. Is my need for status and identity helping the organisation achieve its purpose, or is it there to satisfy a personal desire? If the latter, when does my desire for status and identity result in a conflict between my values and those of the organisation? How do I respond when this occurs? Does this response support the organisation's purpose and values?

Beneath these questions there are even deeper issues to explore when cultivating our self-awareness: What are my deepest desires? What do I really value? How do I fit into this world? It is through slowly developing an understanding of our deepest desires, values and principles that we develop a moral compass that enables us to successfully navigate right versus wrong dilemmas. Those who have not taken the time to develop this level of self-awareness find dealing with ethical dilemmas far more arduous. They can suffer from "stage fright" and paralysis, finding the task of making a decision overwhelming as they have no moral compass to refer to. Alternatively, they can be incoherent and gullible, falling prey to the ideals and opinions of those who surround them. As Alexander Hamilton famously said, "Those who stand for nothing fall for anything."

However, answering these types of questions is no easy task, as they go to the heart of the paradox which is the human condition. We derive meaning by allowing our minds to create superficial identities for ourselves, and a narrative that explains our past and provides for a future full of infinite possibilities. This exercise, despite providing us with much comfort, is ultimately futile, given we are mortal beings. Herein lies the paradox, and why the exercise of exploring our identity can be a terrifying experience, one that we do our utmost to avoid. Deeper contemplation can reveal the limitations of our beliefs, and how the "truth" we have created for ourselves can quickly unravel. As Peter Veenhuizen, a psychologist I know once said to me, "The majority of people go through life with a veil over their face, and they are too scared to remove it because of what they might see."

This being said, there are ways one can work towards a cultivating a deeper understanding of oneself. Psychotherapy is a good place to start. We do not need to have a clinically-diagnosed condition to submit ourselves to psychotherapy. After all, the human condition ensures that we are all neurotic to some degree. A qualified and capable psychotherapist is able to work with us to identify moments when we are using defence mechanisms to protect our fragile ego, and draw this to our attention in a way that makes the discomfort manageable. They are trained to know whether a patient can cope with the veil being ripped off, or whether it needs to be removed gradually over time.

Spiritual practice is also a means by which we can connect with and understand our inner self and most fundamental values. This can take various forms, and does not require us to join an organised religion. For example, journaling and spiritual reading are practices that not only deepen spirituality, but help develop self-awareness and a richer appreciation for the human condition. Mindfulness meditation is a spiritual practice which is now becoming mainstream. Practitioners are said to develop a heightened awareness of the present moment and develop the capacity to focus on their thoughts and emotions in a non-judgemental way. Brain-imaging studies have shown that mindfulness activates brain regions implicated in the process of self-referential thought, suggesting that the positive outcomes associated with it are achieved through the process of disidentification (i.e. a reduced need to build a self-concept and personal identity).[88]

Although insight and awareness are important first steps, one must also have the willingness and desire to make the necessary choices in our lives and organisations that promote ethical behaviour. As George Simon states in his book *In Sheep's Clothing*, this is the "burden of disciplining oneself":[89]

> *To know oneself, to fairly judge one's strengths and weaknesses, and to attain full mastery over one's instincts and inclinations are among life's greatest challenges. Ultimately, anyone's rise to a life of integrity and merit can only come about as the result of a full self-awakening. One must come to know oneself as well as others without deceit or denial. One must honestly face and reckon with all aspects of one's character. Only then can one freely take on the burden of disciplining oneself for one's own sake as well as for the sake of others.*

Research has also shown that even simple measures that enhance self-reflection, like looking into a mirror, can work to decrease unethical behaviour. In a different version of the Halloween trick-or-treat study outlined in chapter two when we were discussing deindividuation, Arthur Beaman and his colleagues placed a mirror on the table containing the treats for the children.[90] When children were asked to only take one treat, the percentage of children taking more than this allocation was significantly higher when the mirror wasn't present. Similarly, in a more recent study conducted by Francesca Gino and Cassie Mogilner, participants were rewarded for their performance on a simple arithmetic task.[91] In conditions when they were availed with the opportunity to cheat, the level of cheating among participants decreased markedly when they completed the task in a cubicle facing a mirror.

Here are 11 questions for senior leaders within any organisation to consider:

1.   Is your organisation connecting you and its employees to a virtuous social purpose?

2.   Have you taken the time to develop an understanding of your personal values and deepest desires?

3.   If so, is there alignment between your life's purpose and values and those of the organisation you work for?

4.   If not, what is driving you to remain at the organisation?

5.   Is there an obsessive, unhealthy focus on performance goals in your organisation?

6.   Is money or other types of financial reward used as a primary motivator in your organisation?

7.   If so, how is it influencing behaviour?

8.   Are you currently seeking a promotion?

9.   If so, is your ambition being driven by a personal desire for status and power, or is the organisation's purpose genuinely better served by you being in a more senior role?

10.   Is poor performance or changes to the organisation's structure making your leadership position unstable?

11.   If so, are you responding defensively and potentially compromising your own or the organisation's values?

Where to Next?

Having covered how context, dysfunctional group dynamics and money, power and fear can act as catalysts for unethical behaviour, the final chapter turns to cognitive biases. The field of behavioural ethics originally emerged from the ideas which appear in the following chapter. From as early as the 1970s, behavioural economists began identifying systemic biases in our cognitions that result in behaviour that is at odds with what would be expected from the rational, self-interested human that underpins most economic theories. Researchers in this field found that at times, human behaviour is quite irrational, as was illustrated earlier in this chapter when discussing the axiom of self-interest. Not only do these biases result in decisions that are at odds with standard economic principles, they can also drive behaviour that is unethical. What's more and as will be illustrated, this can occur without us being aware of it.

Notes

[1]   Smith, A. (1776). *An inquiry into the nature and causes of the wealth of nations.* London, UK: W. Strahan and T. Cadell.

[2]   The reason Adam Smith being labelled as the "founding father" of the axiom of self-interest is undeserving is because he was also acutely aware of man's capacity for altruism. For example, in *The Theory of Moral Sentiments* he wrote:

   How selfish soever man may be supposed, there are evidently some principles in his nature, which interest him in the fortune of others, and render their happiness necessary to him, though he derives nothing from it except the pleasure of seeing it.

[3]   See for example: Becker, G. S. (1978). *The economic approach to human behavior.* Chicago, IL: University of Chicago Press.

[4]   Rubinstein, A. (1982). Perfect equilibrium in a bargaining model. *Econometrica, 50*(1), 97–109.

[5]   Camerer, C., & Thaler, R. H., (1995). Anomalies: Ultimatums, dictators and manners. *The Journal of Economic Perspectives, 9*(2), 209–219.

[6]   Henrich, J., Boyd, R., Bowles, S., Camerer, C., Fehr, E., Gintis, H., ... Tracer, D. (2005). "Economic Man" in cross-cultural perspective: Behavioral experiments in 15 small-scale societies. *Behavioral and Brain Sciences, 28*(6), 795–815.

[7]   Flood, M. M. (1952). *Some experimental games* (Report No. RM-789-1). Santa Monica, CA: RAND.

[8]   Kiyonari, T., Tanida, S., & Yamagishi, T. (2000). Social exchange and reciprocity: Confusion or a heuristic? *Evolution and Human Behavior, 21*(6), 411–427.

[9]   Hayashi, N., Ostrom, E., Walker, J., & Yamagishi, T. (1999). Reciprocity, trust, and the sense of control: A cross-societal study. *Rationality and Society, 11*(1), 27–46.

[10] Andreoni, J., & Miller, J. H. (1993). Rational cooperation in the finitely repeated Prisoner's Dilemma: Experimental evidence. *The Economic Journal, 103*(418), 570–585.

[11] Berkman, E. T., Lukinova, E., Menshikov, I., & Myagkov, M. (2015). Sociality as a natural mechanism of public goods provision. *PLoS One 10*(3), e0119685.

[12] Rilling, J.K., Gutman, D. A., Zeh, T. R., Pagnoni, G., Berns, G. S., & Kilts, C. D. (2002). A neural basis for social cooperation. *Neuron, 35*(2), 395–405.

[13] de Quervain, D. J. F., Fischbacher, U., Treyer, V., Schellhammer, M., Schnyder, U., Buck, A., & Fehr, E. (2004). The neural basis of altruistic punishment. *Science, 305*(5688), 1254–1258.

[14] Tabibnia, G., Satpute, A. B., & Lieberman, M. D. (2010). The sunny side of fairness: Preference for fairness activates reward circuitry (and disregarding unfairness activates self-control circuitry). *Psychological Science, 19*(4), 339–347.

[15] Tricomi, E., Rangel, A., Camerer, C. F., & O'Doherty, J. P. (2010). Neural evidence for inequality-averse social preferences. *Nature, 463*(7284), 1089–1092.

[16] Nowak, M. A. (2006). Five rules for the evolution of cooperation. *Science, 314*(5805), 1560–1563.

[17] Brosnan, S. F., & de Waal, F. B. M. (2003). Monkeys reject unequal pay. *Nature, 425*(6955), 297–299.

[18] I encourage readers to watch Frans de Waal's TED talk that provides video footage of the research – it is very entertaining: de Waal, F. (2011). *Moral behavior in animals* [Video file]. Retrieved December 15, 2015, from http://www.ted.com/talks/frans_de_waal_do_animals_have_morals

[19] Lieberman, M. D. (2013). *Social: Why our brains are wired to connect.* Oxford, UK: Oxford University Press.

[20] Chandor, J. C. (Director), Akers, S., Barnum, R. O., Benaroya, M., Blum, J., Brown, M., Corso, M., Rister, L. (Producers). (2011). *Margin call* [Motion picture]. Los Angeles, CA: Before the Door Pictures & Benaroya Pictures.

[21] Buffet, M., & Clark, D. (2009). *Warren Buffet's management secrets: Proven tools for personal and business success.* London, UK: Simon & Schuster.

[22] Locke, E. A., & Latham, G. P. (2006). New directions in goal-setting theory. *Current Directions in Psychological Science, 15*(5), 265–268.

[23] Simons, D. J., & Chabris, C. F. (1999). Gorillas in our midst: Sustained inattentional blindness for dynamic events. *Perception, 28*(9), 1059–1074.

[24] Neisser, U. (1979). The control of information pickup in selective looking. In A. D. Pick (Ed.), *Perception and its development: A tribute to Eleanor Gibson,* (pp. 201–219). Hillsdale, NJ: Erlbaum.

[25] To watch footage of Daniel Simons discussing the experiment, visit: Bookarmy. (2011, April 18). *The Invisible Gorilla by Chris Chobris and Daniel Simons* [Video file]. Retrieved December 15, 2015, from https://www.youtube.com/watch?v=D_m_9N_3u7o

[26] Staw, B. M., & Boettger, R. D. (1990). Task revision: A neglected form of work performance. *Academy of Management Journal, 33*(3), 534–559.

[27] Johnston, E. (2006, July 5). Calculating traders jailed as judge slams NAB. *The Australian Financial Review,* p. 1.

[28] Grover, S. L., & Hui, C. (2005). How job pressures and extrinsic rewards affect lying behavior. *The International Journal of Conflict Management, 16*(3), 287–300.

[29] Cadsby, C. B., Song, F., & Tapon, F. (2010). Are you paying your employees to cheat? An experimental investigation. *The B. E. Journal of Economic Analysis and Policy, 10*(1), 1–32.

[30] Schweitzer, M. E., Ordóñez, L., & Douma, B. (2004). Goal setting as a motivator of unethical behaviour. *Academy of Management, 47*(3), 422–432.

[31] Jensen, M. C. (2003). Paying people to lie: The truth about the budgeting process. *European Financial Management, 9*(3), 389–406.

[32] Derfus, P. J., Maggitti, P. G., Grimm, C. M., & Smith, K. G. (2008). The Red Queen Effect: Competitive actions and firm performance. *Academy of Management Journal, 51*(1), 61–80.

The phrase "Red Queen Effect" originates from Lewis Carroll's *Through the Looking Glass*, where the character Alice, who is running as fast as she can and realises she is not getting anywhere relative to her surroundings, receives the following response from the Red Queen: "Here, you see, it takes all the running you can do, to keep in the same place. If you want to get somewhere else, you must run at least twice as fast as that!"

[33] Mishina, Y., Dykes, B. J., Block, E. S., & Pollock, T. G. (2010). Why "good" firms do bad things: The effects of high aspirations, high expectation, and prominence on the incidence of corporate illegality. *Academy of Management Journal, 53*(4), 701–722.

[34] Harris, J., & Bromiley, P. (2007). Incentives to cheat: The influence of executive compensation and firm performance on financial misrepresentation. *Organization Science, 18*(3), 350–367.

[35] Heffernan, M. (2011). *Willful blindness: Why we ignore the obvious at our peril*. New York, NY: Walker Publishing Company.

[36] See for example: Prendergast, C. (1999). The provision of incentives in firms. *Journal of Economic Literature, 37*(1), 7–63.

[37] Gino, F., & Pierce, L. (2009). The abundance effect: Unethical behavior in the presence of wealth. *Organizational Behavior and Human Decisions Processes, 109*(2), 142–155.

[38] Arnold, M., Goff, S., & Parker, G. (2014, February 11). Barclays under fire on pay amid job cuts. *Financial Times*. Retrieved December 15, 2015, from http://www.ft.com/intl/cms/s/0/373c4d50-92ea-11e3-b07c-00144feab7de.html#slide0

[39] Luttmer, E. F. P. (2005). Neighbors as negatives: Relative earnings and well-being. *The Quarterly Journal of Economics, 120*(3), 963-1002; Solnicka, S. J., & Hemenway, D. (1998). Is more always better? A survey on positional concerns. *Journal of Economic Behavior and Organization, 37*(3), 373–383.

[40] Breiter, H. C., Aharon, I., Kahneman, D., Dale, A., & Shizgal, P. (2001). Functional imaging of neural responses to expectancy and experience of monetary gains and losses. *Neuron, 30*(2), 619–639; Knutson, B., Fong, G. W., Adams, C. M., Varner, J. L., & Hommer, D. (2001). Dissociation of reward anticipation and outcome with event-related fRMI. *Neuroreport, 12*(17), 3683–3687.

[41] Harvey, A. H., Kirk, U., Denfield, G. H., & Montague, P. R. (2010). Monetary favors and their influence on neural responses and revealed preference. *The Journal of Neuroscience, 30*(28), 9597–9602.

[42] Cain, D. M., Loewenstein, G., & Moore, D. A. (2005). The dirt on coming clean: Perverse effects of disclosing conflicts of interest. *Journal of Legal Studies, 34*(1), 1–25.

[43] Vohs, K, D., Mead, N. L., & Goode, M. R. (2006). The psychological consequences of money. *Science, 314*(5802), 1154–1156.

[44] Pink, D. H. (2009). *Drive: The surprising truth about what motivates us.* London, UK: Riverhead Books.

[45] Ariely, D., Gneezy, U., Loewenstein, G., & Mazar, N. (2009). Large stakes and big mistakes. *The Review of Economic Studies, 76*(2), 451–469.

[46] Glucksberg, S. (1962). The influence of strength of drive on functional fixedness and perceptual recognition. *Journal of Experimental Psychology, 63*(1), 36–41.

[47] Duncker, K. (1945). On problem solving. *Psychological Monographs, 58*(270), i–113.

[48] For two recent examples see: Chemi, E., & Giorgi, A. (2014, July 22). The pay-for-performance myth. *Bloomberg Businessweek.* Retrieved December 15, 2015, from http://www.bloomberg.com/bw/articles/2014-07-22/for-ceos-correlation-between-pay-and-stock-performance-is-pretty-random; Kohler, A. (2013, July 31). The myth of pay for performance. *Business Spectator.* Retrieved December 15, 2015, from http://www.businessspectator.com.au/article/2013/7/31/financial-services/myth-pay-performance

[49] Heyman, J., & Ariely, D. (2004). Effort for payment: A tale of two markets. *Psychological Science, 15*(11), 787–793.

[50] Mellström, C., & Johannesson. M. (2008). Crowding out in blood donation: Was Titmuss right? *Journal of the European Economic Association, 6*(4), 845–863.

[51] Gneezy, U., & Rustichini, A. (2000). A fine is a price. *The Journal of Legal Studies, 29*(1), 1–17.

[52] Grant, A. M., Campbell, E. M., Chen, G., Cottone, K., Lapedis, D., & Lee, K. (2007). Impact and the art of motivation maintenance: The effects of contact with beneficiaries on persistence behaviour. *Organizational Behavior and Human Decision Processes, 103*(1), 53–67.

[53] Carney, M. J. (2014, May 27). *Inclusive capitalism: Creating a sense of the systemic.* Speech given at the Conference of Inclusive Capitalism, London, UK. Retrieved December 15, 2015, from http://www.bankofengland.co.uk/publications/Pages/speeches/2014/731.aspx

[54] Cohen, L. N. (1985). Hallelujah. On *Various positions* [CD]. New York, NY: Columbia Records.

[55] Badaracco, J. L. (2006). *Questions of character.* Boston, MA: Harvard Business School Publishing.

[56] Ludwig, D. C., & Longenecker, C. O. (1993). The Bathsheba Syndrome: The ethical failure of successful leaders. *Journal of Business Ethics, 12*(4), 265–273.

[57] Kipnis, D. (1972). Does power corrupt? *Journal of Personality and Social Psychology, 24*(1), 33–41.

[58] Bendahan, S., Zehnder, C., Pralong, F. P., & Antonakis, J. (2015). Leader corruption depends on power and testosterone. *The Leadership Quarterly, 26*(2), 101–122.

[59] Galinsky, A. D., Gruenfeld, D. H., & Magee, J. C. (2003). From power to action. *Journal of Personality and Social Psychology, 85*(3), 453–466.

[60] Keltner, D., Gruenfeld, D., & Anderson, C. (2003). Power, approach, and inhibition. *Psychological Review, 110*(2), 265–284.

[61] Galinsky, A. D., Gruenfeld, D. H., & Magee, J. C. (2003).

[62] Pitesa, M., & Thau, S. (2013). Compliant sinners, obstinate saints: How power and self-focus determine the effectiveness of social influences in ethical decision making. *Academy of Management Journal, 56*(3), 635–658.

[63] Galinsky, A. D., Magee, J. C., Gruenfeld, D. H., Whiston, J. A., & Liljenquist, K. A. (2008). Power reduces the press of the situation: Implications for creativity, conformity, and dissonance. *Journal of Personality and Social Psychology, 95*(6), 1450–1466.

[64] Guinote, A. (2008). Power and affordances: When the situation has more power over powerful than powerless individuals. *Journal of Personality and Social Psychology, 95*(2), 237–252.

[65] Overbeck, J., & Park, B. (2006). Powerful perceivers, powerless objects: Flexibility of power-holders' social attention. *Organizational Behavior and Human Decision Processes, 99*(2), 227–243.

[66] Gruenfeld, D. H., Inesi, M. E., Magee, J. C., & Galinsky, A. D. (2008). Power and the objectification of social targets. *Journal of Personality and Social Psychology, 95*(1), 111–127.

[67] Virato, S. (1993, November). The Tibetan Book of Living & Dying: A dialogue with Sogyal Rinpoche with Swami Virato. *New Frontier*. Retrieved December 15, 2015, from http://www.sacred-texts.com/bud/tib/living.htm

[68] Fast, N. J., & Chen, S. (2009). When the boss feels inadequate: Power, incompetence, and aggression. *Psychological Science, 20*(11), 1406–1413.

[69] Leary, M. R., Terry, M. L., Allen, A. B., & Tate, E. B. (2009). The concept of ego threat in social and personality psychology: Is ego threat a viable scientific construct? *Personality and Social Psychology Review, 13*(3), 151–164.

[70] Zuckerman, M. (1979). Attribution of success and failure revisited, or: The motivational bias is alive and well in attribution theory. *Journal or Personality, 47*(2), 245–287.

[71] Mischel, W., Ebbesen, E. B., & Zeiss, A. R. (1976). Determinants of selective memory about the self. *Journal of Consulting and Clinical Psychology, 44*(1), 92–103.

[72] Wills, T. A. (1981). Downward comparison principles in social psychology. *Psychological Bulletin, 90*(2), 245–271.

[73] Alicke, M. D. (1985). Global self-evaluation as determined by the desirability and controllability of trait adjectives. *Journal of Personality and Social Psychology, 49*(6), 1621–1630.

[74] Dunning, D., Perie, M., & Story, A. L. (1991). Self-serving prototypes of social categories. *Journal of Personality and Social Psychology, 61*(6), 957–968.

[75] Ditto, P. H., & Boardman, A. F. (1995). Perceived accuracy of favorable and unfavorable psychological feedback. *Basic and Applied Social Psychology, 16*(1–2), 137–157.

[76] Kruger, J., & Dunning, D. (1999). Unskilled and unaware of it: How difficulties in recognizing one's own incompetence lead to inflated self-assessments. *Journal of Personal and Social Psychology, 77*(6), 1121–1134.

[77] Izuma, K., Saito, D. N., & Sadato, N. (2008). Processing of social and monetary rewards in the human striatum. *Neuron, 58*(2), 284–294.

[78] Vignoles, V. L., Regalia, C., Manzi, C., Golledge, J., & Scabini, E. (2006). Beyond self-esteem: Influence of multiple motives on identity construction. *Journal of Personality and Social Psychology, 90*(2), 308–333.

[79] Brunell, A. B., Gentry, W. A., Campbell, W. K., Hoffman, B. J., Kuhnert, K. W., & DeMarree, K. G. (2008). Leader emergence: The case of the narcissistic leader. *Personality and Social Psychology Bulletin, 34*(12), 1663–1676.

[80] Moore, C., Wakeman, S. W., & Gino, F. (2014). *Dangerous expectations: Breaking rules to resolve cognitive dissonance.* (Working Paper No. 15-012). Boston, MA: Harvard Business School. Retrieved December 15, 2015, from http://www.hbs.edu/faculty/Publication%20Files/15-012_02b51f56-9ad4-46a5-9195-90d1852ac95d.pdf

[81]   Georgesen, J., & Harris, M. J. (2006). Holding onto power: Effects of powerholders' positional instability and expectancies on interactions with subordinates. *European Journal of Social Psychology, 36*(4), 451–468.

[82]   Greenberg, J., & Arndt, J. (2011). Terror management theory. In P. A. M. Van Lange, A. W. Kruglanski, & T. E. Higgins (Eds.), *Handbook of theories of social psychology* (Vol. 1, pp. 398–415). London, UK: SAGE Publications.

[83]   Rinpoche, S. (2002). *The Tibetan book of living and dying.* New York, NY: HarperCollins Publishers.

[84]   Becker, E. (1973). *The denial of death.* New York, NY: The Free Press.

[85]   Pyszczynski, T., Greenberg, J., Solomon, S., Arndt, J., & Schimel, J. (2004). Why do people need self-esteem? A theoretical and empirical review. *Psychological Bulletin, 130*(3), 435–468.

[86]   Mandel, N., & Heine, S. J. (1999). Terror management and marketing: He who dies with the most toys wins. *Advances in Consumer Research, 26*(1), 527–532.

[87]   Heine, S. J., Harihara, M., & Niiya, Y. (2002). Terror management in Japan. *Asian Journal of Social Psychology, 5*(3), 187–196.

[88]   Ives-Deliperi, V. L., Solms, M., & Meintjes, E. M. (2011). The neural substrates of mindfulness: An fMRI investigation. *Social Neuroscience, 6*(3), 231–242.

[89]   Simon, G. K. (1996). *In sheep's clothing: Understanding and dealing with manipulative people.* Little Rock, AR: Parkhurst Brothers Publising.

[90]   Beaman, A. L., Klentz, B., Diener, E., & Svanum, S. (1979). Self-awareness and transgression in children: Two field studies. *Journal of Personality and Social Psychology, 37*(10), 1835–1846.

[91]   Gino, F., & Mogilner, C. (2014). Time, money and morality. *Psychological Science, 25*(2), 414–421.

What We Fail to See

Blindness

We can be blind to the obvious, and we are also blind to our blindness.[1]

Daniel Kahneman, Thinking Fast and Slow

In recent times, a dual process theory of the mind has emerged which suggests that humans employ two distinct processing mechanisms when engaging in a task.[2] More recently made famous in Daniel Kahneman's book *Thinking Fast and Slow*,[3] the theory proposes that there are two modes of human thought, most often referred to as System 1 and System 2. System 1 thinking is said to operate automatically and non-consciously, with little effort and no sense of control. System 2 thinking meanwhile involves conscious, effortful thought, and is the type of methodical thinking engaged when completing complex computations. It is often said that System 2 thinking is unique to humans, enabling us to undertake abstract thinking.

Some scholars have proposed an evolutionary explanation for this model of human cognition, and it is easy to see how it is adaptive. System 1 thinking ensured no time was wasted and quick decisions were made when our ancestors were being chased by a sabre-toothed tiger. On the other hand, the analysis and thought enabled by System 2 thinking provided us with the ability to solve the complex problems associated with building communities and civilisations. However, in some cases we automatically engage System 1 thinking to solve problems and make decisions that require deeper thought. In these instances, we can, without conscious awareness, behave in ways that are not only irrational but also unethical. The term "bounded ethicality" has been coined by some academics to describe this propensity for us to engage cognitive processes that cause us to behave unethically without being aware of it.[4]

In support of this approach, Jonathan Haidt recently developed a social intuitionist model of moral reasoning to help explain many of the recent findings suggesting that we do not adopt a rational approach when making decisions with moral consequence.[5] The model posits that social and cultural factors play a far more important role in moral reasoning than personal reflection. More importantly, it suggests that moral judgment is intuitive and heavily biased towards rapid, automatic processes, rather than slow thoughtful ones. Moral reasoning is engaged post hoc to provide rational justifications for decisions made. In support of this model, Joshua Greene and his colleagues have shown that for certain types of moral dilemmas, brain regions responsible for abstract reasoning and dealing with cognitive conflict and control are not activated.[6]

This chapter outlines some of the biases in our decision making that the cognitive processes associated with System 1 thinking can create and how they can lead to unethical behaviour. The intention is not to provide a thorough review of all the known biases – there are other excellent books that fulfil this purpose.[7] However, the focus will be on the biases that I believe played a central role in the FX trading scandal at the NAB. We begin with the slippery slope, which illustrates how gradual erosions in our ethical standards can go unnoticed.

The Slippery Slope

> *Indeed the safest road to Hell is the gradual one – the gentle slope, soft underfoot, without sudden turnings, without milestones, without signposts ...*[8]

C. S. *Lewis*, The Screwtape Letters

Most of us would be familiar with the parable of the boiling frog. The story goes that if a frog is placed in boiling water, it will detect the threat and jump out. However, if a frog is placed in cool water that is gradually heated up, it will not detect the change in temperature and eventually die when the water reaches boiling point.[9] The slippery slope of decision making works on a similar premise. Namely, an individual or organisation will be more willing to behave in a manner considered grossly unethical if it has been preceded by a series of similar but smaller ethical transgressions. These smaller ethical transgressions act as a benchmark, and anchor the ethical standards applied to subsequent decisions.

In a recent study investigating the slippery slope of decision making, Francesca Gino and Max Bazerman cleverly illustrated how people are more likely to sanction unethical behaviour when it degrades gradually, rather than abruptly.[10] In their research, Gino and Bazerman had participants view a series of jars filled with US one cent pieces. Their role was to either approve or reject an estimate of the amount of money in the jar provided by the "estimator" (unbeknown to the participants, the estimates were provided by the experimenters). Participants knew that the estimators were conflicted, as they were rewarded when high estimates were approved, thus providing them with an incentive to inflate their estimates. Meanwhile, the participants were also rewarded for approving high estimates, but risked a penalty when inflated estimates were approved.

The participants were split into two groups, an "abrupt change" group and a "slippery slope" group. Table 4.1 shows the estimates that the participants had to approve or reject over 16 rounds, including the actual amount of money that was in the jar in each round. As can be seen, in the abrupt change group, the estimates are equal to the actual amount of money in the jar up to round 11, at which point there is a sudden jump in the value provided by the estimator. In the slippery slope group meanwhile, there is a gradual increase in the value of the estimates up to round 11, after which the estimates are identical to those provided to the participants in the abrupt change group. Gino and Bazerman were interested in the decisions that participants made between rounds 11 and 16 inclusive, where both sets of participants faced the same choices.

The findings showed that participants in the slippery slope group were far more likely to approve the inflated estimates provided in rounds 11 to 16. Aggregating the rate of approval across these final six rounds, participants approved 52 per cent of the estimates in the slippery slope group, while only 24 per cent of the estimates were approved in the abrupt change group. What's more, Gino and Bazerman found evidence to suggest that the participants in the slippery slope group not only did not notice the gradual exaggeration of the estimates, but also, unlike the participants in the abrupt change group, did not feel that the estimates were unethical.

In all of the well-publicised ethical failures, it is always the case that the unethical behaviour underpinning the incidents evolved and degraded over time. Professional cycling did not move from a position where one day the

Table 4.1   The estimates of the amount of money in the jar that
             participants were required to accept or reject. As can be
             seen, for rounds 11 to 16 inclusive, the estimates provided
             were identical

Round	Slippery slope group	Abrupt change group	Actual amount of money in jar
1	$10.01	$10.01	$10.01
2	$10.37	$9.97	$9.97
3	$10.84	$10.04	$10.04
4	$11.21	$10.01	$10.01
5	$11.58	$9.98	$9.98
6	$12.00	$10.00	$10.00
7	$12.44	$10.04	$10.04
8	$12.79	$9.99	$9.99
9	$13.22	$10.02	$10.02
10	$13.59	$9.99	$9.99
11	$14.02	$14.02	$10.02
12	$14.01	$14.01	$10.01
13	$13.98	$13.98	$9.98
14	$13.99	$13.99	$9.99
15	$14.02	$14.02	$10.02
16	$14.03	$14.03	$10.03

Source: Gino, F., & Bazerman, M. H. (2009). When misconduct goes unnoticed: The acceptability of gradual erosion in others' ethical behavior. *Journal of Experimental Social Psychology, 45*(4), 708–719.

peloton was clean, and the next day the use of performance-enhancing drugs was endemic and openly spoken about. Similarly in the LIBOR rate-fixing scandal, employees at financial institutions were not providing unbiased estimates of the key benchmark rates on one day, and the following day coming to work and speaking openly over taped phone lines about manipulating these same benchmark rates. Typically, ethical failures begin with a minor transgression that in of itself may not appear unethical. The slippery slope illustrates how this initial transgression can erode over time, resulting in both individuals and organisations significantly compromising their ethical standards.

The FX trading incident at the NAB classically illustrated the slippery slope in action. Not only did ethical standards erode over time, but the seriousness of the ethical transgressions accelerated – the slippery slope is indeed slippery.

Initially, the true value of the currency options portfolio was misstated to "smooth" the earnings profile of the business, but the line between "smoothing" and hiding losses was clearly breached at some point.[11]

Firstly, the techniques used to conceal the true value of portfolio evolved over time, trending towards more sinister methods as the losses mounted. A report into the incident found that losses were concealed using the following principal methods:

- Recording incorrect rates on genuine spot foreign exchange transactions (initiated at some stage in 2001).

- Entering fictitious spot foreign exchange transactions with incorrect rates (initiated at some stage in 2003).

- Entering fictitious foreign exchange option transactions (initiated in late 2003).

Furthermore, the true value of the portfolio was misstated for some time to conceal the true financial position of the business. However, as Table 4.2 illustrates, the degree to which the value of the portfolio was overstated grew over time and accelerated in the months prior to the losses being exposed.

Table 4.2   Amount of overstatement in the value of the currency options portfolio at the National Australia Bank

Period ending	Approximate overstatement of portfolio value (AUD)
September 2001	$4.2 million
September 2002	$8.0 million
September 2003	$42.0 million
January 2004	$360.0 million

Source: PricewaterhouseCoopers. (2004, March 12). Investigation into foreign exchange losses at the National Australia Bank. Melbourne, Australia: Author.

Finally, the risk limits[12] within which the business was supposed to operate were not only consistently breached throughout 2003, but as Figure 4.1 illustrates, the size of the breaches accelerated towards the end of that year.

The slippery slope provides a plausible explanation for why the financial position of the currency options business deteriorated over time and also why

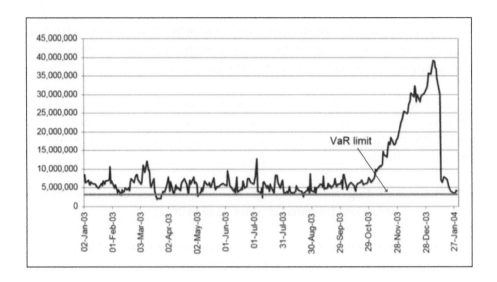

**Figure 4.1   National Australia Bank currency options portfolio Value at
                 Risk, January 2003 to January 2004**

Source: PricewaterhouseCoopers. (2004, March 12).

the methods employed to hide losses became more sinister. However, there
are other biases in our cognitions driven by System 1 thinking that can provide
a plausible explanation for these trends. These are loss aversion, framing
and overconfidence.

Loss Aversion and Framing

> *Every mile is two in winter.*
>
>   *George Herbert,* Jacula Prudentum

The following dilemma (or derivatives of it) is arguably one of the most widely
cited in decision making courses at modern business schools:[13]

> *Imagine that the U.S. is preparing for the outbreak of an unusual Asian
> disease, which is expected to kill 600 people. Two alternative programs
> to combat the disease have been proposed.*

Amos Tversky and Daniel Kahneman presented this problem to two
groups. The first group, which contained 152 people, was provided with the
following information:

Assume that the exact scientific estimate of the consequences of the programs are as follows:

Program A
If Program A is adopted, 200 people will be saved.

Program B
If Program B is adopted, there is a one third probability that 600 people will be saved, and two thirds probability that no people will be saved.

When faced with the above choices, 72 per cent selected programme A, while 28 per cent selected programme B.

The second group contained 155 people and was provided with the following information:

Program C
If Program C is adopted 400 people will die.

Program D
If Program D is adopted there is a one third probability that nobody will die, and a two thirds probability that 600 people will die.

When faced with the above choices, 22 per cent selected programme C, while 78 per cent selected programme D.

The astute reader will have noticed that the outcomes associated with programmes A and C are identical, as are the outcomes associated with programmes B and D. Yet when presented to two different groups, the majority preferences seem to suggest that the outcomes associated with programmes A and C and programmes B and D are dramatically different. With this simple problem, Tversky and Kahneman eloquently illustrated two of the classic shortcomings associated with System 1 thinking, namely loss aversion and the framing effect. We begin by exploring loss aversion and how it can be a driver of unethical conduct.

LOSS AVERSION

In the above "Asian disease" problem, programmes A and B were presented in terms of "lives saved" whereas programmes C and D were presented in terms of "lives lost". People respond very differently when confronting gains compared to when they are confronting losses, a central tenant of prospect theory. Prospect theory was developed by Tversky and Kahneman and provides a model for how people make decisions in conditions of uncertainty.[14] It revolutionised how we think about decision making under risk and challenged many of the ideas underpinning expected utility theory, a theory which prior to the development of prospect theory dominated thinking in this area.

One of the key departures from expected utility theory that prospect theory proposed is how people value gains and losses. Essentially, successive gains are valued at a decreasing rate, while the displeasure associated with losses also decreases as they increase. However, the response to losses is far more extreme than that for gains, such that the displeasure associated with losing a sum of money is far greater than the pleasure associated with gaining the same amount (hence the term "loss aversion").

This pattern of responses to gains and losses has been illustrated in countless studies, and it also helps explain the inconsistent responses to the Asian disease problem. When the programmes to combat the disease were framed as a loss (programmes C and D), people were more likely to select the programme that contained an element of risk (programme D). However, when the programmes were framed as gains (programmes A and B), the tendency was to select the option that provided greater certainty (programme A). More recently, researchers have also shown how this pattern of responses applies to ethical judgment.

Mary Kern and Dolly Chugh conducted a series of studies that illustrated how people have a tendency to respond in a less ethical manner when a decision is presented in a loss frame compared to when it is presented in a gain frame.[15] In one of their studies, participants were placed in pairs and asked to play the role of agents for the buyer or seller of a family property. The seller was only interested in selling the property to someone who would put it to "tasteful use", while the buyer's agent was representing a developer of high-rise hotels. In addition to being instructed not to reveal the buyer's identity or the intended use of the property, the buyer's agent was also told that they would receive a 3 per cent commission. When the likelihood of the property being sold was presented in a loss frame ("you have a 75 per cent chance of losing this property, and thus your commission") the buyer's agent lied more about their client's intentions and reported being more dishonest than when the likelihood of a sale was presented in a gain frame ("you have a 25 per cent chance of gaining this property, and thus your commission").

This aversion to losses provides another explanation for why the risk profile of the currency options business at the NAB evolved the way it did towards the end of the 2003 calendar year. As the amount of losses being carried increased (Table 4.2), so too did the level of risk taking (Figure 4.1). I would hazard a guess that if the value of the portfolio was being understated and gains as opposed to losses were being carried, then the risk profile would not have grown exponentially.

In chapter three, we discussed how it is not uncommon for leaders to engage in defensive behaviour when the hold on their positions becomes tenuous or is under threat. Arguably loss aversion also provides an alternative explanation for this conduct. As explained, there is so much at stake for leaders when their roles appear terminal – status, prestige, lucrative financial rewards, career, lifestyle, and ultimately their self-concept and identity. Under these circumstances, it is little wonder that leaders engage in defensive and at times unethical behaviour – there is so much to lose.

FRAMING

The way in which dilemmas are presented to us has a profound effect on how we view them and the types of decisions we ultimately make. In the "Asian disease" problem for example, presenting programmes in terms of "lives saved" as opposed to "lives lost" resulted in very different decisions. Although in the academic literature the concept of framing is traditionally associated with gains and losses, the effect stretches beyond this context. For example, framing effects have also been shown to operate when decisions are framed to be of a "business" nature or of an "ethical" nature.

In a study using the Prisoner's Dilemma Game, Varda Liberman and her colleagues recruited participants after they were nominated by a peer to be either (a) most likely to act in a cooperative manner ("most likely to cooperate"), or (b) most likely to act in a competitive manner ("most likely to defect").[16] After being recruited, participants were paired in such a way that both players in the dyad were either most likely to cooperate or most likely to defect. With their partner, they then took part in a seven-trial Prisoner's Dilemma Game that provided monetary payoffs. In addition to dividing the participants according to their perceived level of cooperativeness and competitiveness, Liberman and her colleagues also changed the labelling of the game. For some of the pairs the game was referred to as the "Wall Street Game", while for others it was referred to as the "Community Game".

As the results in Figure 4.2 illustrate, the disposition of the participant as predicted by their peers (cooperate or defect) had little influence on how they chose to respond in the Prisoner's Dilemma Game. Far more telling was the labelling provided to the game. In the first round of the "Community Game", 67 per cent of the participants who were selected on the basis that they were cooperators and 75 per cent of the participants who were selected on the basis that they would defect chose to cooperate. Meanwhile in the "Wall Street Game", 33 per cent of the participants chose to cooperate in the first round of the game regardless of their predicted disposition. Across the seven trials of the game, the pattern of results was very similar.

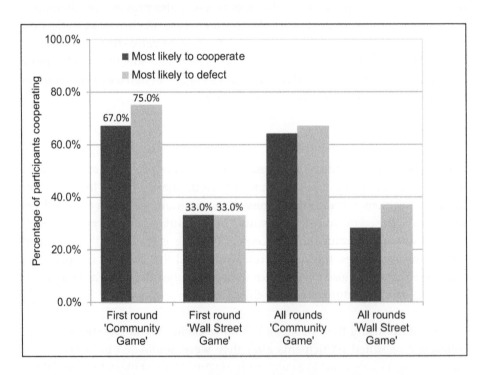

Figure 4.2   **Percentage of cooperative responses in the first round and across all seven trials of the "Community Game" and the "Wall Street Game". Participants played the game in pairs, where both members of the pair were selected on the basis that they were more likely to "cooperate" or more likely to "defect"**

Source: Liberman, V., Samuels, S. M., & Ross, L. (2004). The name of the game: Predictive power of reputations versus situational labels in determining Prisoner's Dilemma Game moves. *Personality and Social Psychology Bulletin, 30*(9), 1175–1185.

Although the above study illustrates the effects of framing, the parallels with the key lessons provided in chapter one should not be overlooked. Firstly, relying on reputation or character assessments to predict how someone will behave in certain situations can lead to spurious and inaccurate assessments of future behaviour. Secondly, we drastically underestimate how the context within which we operate can profoundly effect our behaviour. Even the most subtle environmental cues can cause someone considered to be selfless, fair and cooperative to behave in a competitive, self-interested manner. As Liberman and her colleagues noted, the use of the labels "Wall Street Game" and "Community Game" activated the presence of different social norms:

> *The former label ["Wall Street Game"], of course, connotes rugged individualism, concern with self-interest, and contexts in which competitive or exploitative norms are likely to operate. The latter label ["Community Game"], by contrast, connotes interdependence, collective interest, and contexts wherein cooperative norms are likely to operate.*

Perhaps even more pernicious are results from research undertaken by Ann Tenbrunsel and David Messick that illustrated how the imposition of regulations or sanctions can cause people to frame a problem as one requiring a "business" decision rather than an "ethical" decision.[17] In their study, participants were put in a hypothetical scenario in which they were running a manufacturing plant that emitted toxic gases. The dilemma they faced represented a public goods dilemma, as they were asked to use a device at a cost that would reduce the emissions of the toxic gases to a level acceptable to the authorities. However, they also knew that if other manufacturers complied, they could potentially get away without using the device themselves.

Tenbrunsel and Messick found that when sanctions were applied (the increased likelihood of inspections), participants were more likely to view the decisions to use the device as a "business" decision rather than an "ethical" decision. Furthermore, this framing reduced the level of compliance among participants who were assigned with the sanctions. More recent research undertaken by Maryam Kouchaki and her colleagues showed that priming participants to think about money also activated this "business" decision frame, and drove increased unethical behaviour.[18] This latter finding is hardly surprising, given the discussion about reward in chapter three.

The role that framing plays in driving unethical behaviour in the business world cannot be underestimated. It is so often the case that the ethical dimension of the decisions we make are overlooked, not because we are unethical people, but because the issue at hand has been presented in a way that makes it appear as if it is a commercial decision with no ethical consequences. Recall in chapter two how the Ford Motor Company made a decision not to proceed with a safer design for their Pinto on the basis of a commercial "cost/benefit" analysis. As will be discussed in the conclusion to this chapter, leaders should ensure the ethical dimensions of a decision are always considered during deliberation. At the risk of sounding like a broken record, arguably the most effective way of making this happen is by connecting leaders to a virtuous purpose and the social responsibilities associated with their roles.

In addition to the slippery slope, loss aversion and the framing effect, there is one final decision making bias associated with System 1 thinking that can explain the trading activity associated with the FX trading scandal at the NAB – overconfidence.

Overconfidence

> It is also true that the less competent a person is in a given domain, the more he will tend to overestimate his abilities. This often produces an ugly marriage of confidence and ignorance that is very difficult to correct for.[19]

> *Sam Harris,* The Moral Landscape

In many ways related to our need for self-esteem, human beings are overconfident. As with most of the biases in our cognitive processes associated with System 1 thinking, overconfidence is a double-edged sword. On the one hand, it can easily be seen how overconfidence has evolutionary value – it enables us to forge ahead, even if the odds are stacked against us. On the other hand, overconfidence can drive less than ideal outcomes. A classic illustration of how overconfidence can drive unethical conduct in the business world was provided by Catherine Schrand and Sarah Zechman.[20] In an investigation into financial misreporting in the US during the 1990s and 2000s, they found evidence for a relationship between executive overconfidence about future performance and income misrepresentation. They provide the following summary to describe how this pattern of behaviour evolves:

> *A manager with unrealistic (optimistic) expectations about future earnings realizations is more likely to underestimate the need for more*

egregious earnings management in future periods. Thus, when he faces
a shortfall, he is more likely to manage earnings in a minor amount and
start down the slippery slope to fraud. In turn, he is more likely to be
in the position where egregious earnings management is the optimal
choice in a subsequent period.

The pioneering studies into overconfidence asked participants to answer a series of general knowledge questions with two alternative responses and provide a probability of their answer being correct.[21] Participants in these studies were generally overconfident – their assigned probabilities were greater than the actual proportion of correct responses. This being said, a pattern also emerged in that people were most overconfident when the items were more difficult and there was greater uncertainty. As the level of difficulty decreased, so did the level of overconfidence, with underconfidence emerging for extremely easy items.

Given this pattern of results, it is no surprise that this tendency towards overconfidence reigns supreme in the world of financial markets, as it is an arena that is punctuated by high uncertainty and volatility. Retail investors are particularly prone to allowing overconfidence make them believe that their knowledge and skill will enable them to outperform the market. Comprehensive studies of trading activity have shown that when retail investors engage in active trading strategies, they generate inferior returns.[22] Meanwhile, professional investors, despite having access to superior resources and information, don't fare much better. In my experience, they fail one of the most basic tests of ability: consistent year-on-year outperformance.[23]

There are several biases associated with System 1 thinking that help fuel overconfidence among investors in financial markets. One is confirmation bias. Since the seminal study conducted by Charles Lord and his colleagues in 1979, there is now copious research illustrating our tendency to not only selectively seek out information that is aligned to our existing views, but also distort or refute information that challenges our opinions.[24] It has been proposed that a key driver of confirmation bias is our desire to reduce the cognitive dissonance associated with finding evidence that challenges our views and opinions.

In a study undertaken by JaeHong Park and his colleagues, the online activity of investors visiting a portal providing news, information, pricing and recommendations on the stock market was analysed.[25] The study found that not only did investors seek out opinions that were aligned with their existing views, but this tendency was more pronounced the stronger the view they held. Furthermore, in addition to exhibiting greater confirmation bias, investors with stronger views also displayed overconfidence in their trading patterns, engaging in higher trading frequency which ultimately led to inferior returns.

A second bias that helps fuel overconfidence is the self-serving bias, a concept mentioned in chapter three when discussing the human desire to enhance and protect self-esteem. The bias refers to our propensity to take personal credit for positive outcomes and attribute negative outcomes to external factors. In an analysis of the trading activity of mutual funds in the US between 1985 and 2006, Darwin Choi and Dong Lou found evidence suggesting that active fund managers display self-serving bias.[26] As Choi and Lou state:

> Investors in financial markets are particularly susceptible to the self-serving attribution bias, as investment decisions can only be verified with vague and delayed feedbacks.

Choi and Lou found that whenever active fund managers achieved returns above benchmark, they showed a tendency to self-attribute outperformance. In addition, the overconfidence this self-attribution engendered resulted in the fund managers taking positions in industries that they were not familiar with, providing an explanation for why they tended to underperform their peers in subsequent periods.

Finally, overconfidence can also be fuelled by the illusion of control. This bias was classically illustrated by a series of studies conducted by Ellen Langer.[27] Using a variety of tasks whose outcomes were determined totally by chance, Langer was able to illustrate that participants perceived a degree of control over the outcome when certain cues were introduced that suggested an element of skill was required. For example, in one of the studies, if the participants were able to choose their lottery ticket, they were less willing to exchange it for a ticket they couldn't choose, even though it provided them with entry into a lottery where the odds of winning were higher. In another study, participants believed they were more likely to win a game of chance when they were competing against an opponent who did not appear to be capable.

As outlined by Mark Fenton-O'Creevy and his colleagues, the trading environment in financial markets provides a perfect environment for a trader to develop an illusion of control, as it is very difficult to ascertain whether an outcome is the result of a trader's decision and skill or pure chance.[28] Furthermore, as the self-serving bias shows us, traders are very adept at establishing causal relationships between positive outcomes and their decisions.

In totality, the above research demonstrates that success in financial markets is less about skill and more about chance, yet traders have an uncanny ability to make us believe otherwise. In volatile, low-validity environments where there is a lot of uncertainty, System 1 thinking is able to create coherence and order where none exists, enabling us to create bogus narratives that link a random epoch of outperformance to superior skill or knowledge. In the famous words of Philip Tetlock, "experts are poorer at predictions than dart-throwing monkeys".

Before turning to the lessons for leaders, we will explore the concept of moral disengagement. Although moral disengagement is not attributed to the shortcomings associated with System 1 thinking, it is a theory that provides an explanation for how individuals modify their beliefs and attitudes to avoid any cognitive dissonance associated with questionable and immoral conduct. At the extreme, moral disengagement allows us to create an illusion that we are behaving morally when we are in fact not.

Moral Disengagement

> *Moral justification is a powerful disengagement mechanism. Destructive conduct is made personally and socially acceptable by portraying it in the service of moral ends.*[29]

> *Albert Bandura*

Moral disengagement is a theory developed by Albert Bandura, who, as we saw in chapter one, also developed social learning theory. It proposes that the adoption of moral standards is not a sufficient safeguard against questionable conduct. Rather, there are numerous mechanisms that act to engage (or disengage) our ability to self-regulate. If these mechanisms work to compromise our ability to self-regulate, then one can behave in a manner that is at odds with their moral standards and not experience any distress or guilt in the process.

In a study conducted by Lisa Shu and her colleagues, the role moral disengagement plays in making unethical behaviour permissible was cleverly illustrated.[30] Firstly, asking participants to contemplate behaving unethically by cheating on an exam activated moral disengagement. Secondly, moral disengagement was found to increase when participants were placed in a permissive environment and provided with the opportunity to cheat in a problem-solving task. Finally, not only did participants provided with the opportunity to cheat behave more dishonestly, but moral disengagement also led to "motivated forgetting" – these participants recalled fewer items of an honour code they read prior to completing the problem-solving task. Meanwhile, a more recent study conducted by Celia Moore and her colleagues showed that reporting to an ethical leader is a safeguard against moral disengagement.[31]

Bandura proposed that moral disengagement occurs through a set of eight mechanisms.[32] Aspects of two of these have already been discussed in chapter two, namely obedience to authority (what Bandura referred to as *displacement of responsibility*) and the bystander effect (what Bandura referred to as *diffusion of responsibility*). Although the remaining six mechanisms are not all explored here, three are particularly relevant both to my experience and other incidents of ethical failures in the business world – euphemistic labelling, advantageous comparison and distortion of consequences.

EUPHEMISTIC LABELLING

The power of language cannot be underestimated. This was illustrated in the study discussed above where Liberman and her colleagues showed that simply changing the label assigned to the Prisoner's Dilemma Game ("Wall Street Game" or "Community Game") profoundly influenced behaviour. Euphemistic labelling refers to how language can make totally inappropriate conduct appear respectable and also work to relieve people of any guilt associated with their unethical conduct.

Examples abound of where the labelling applied to unethical behaviour can sanitise the conduct and make it appear appropriate. Professional cyclists were not "riding without the assistance of performance-enhancing drugs", they were "riding paniagua". In the LIBOR rate-fixing scandal, traders were not "manipulating the true value of the six-month benchmark rate", they were asking for "high 6M fix". To cover shortfalls in operating results between 2002 and 2006, Dell was not "manipulating its income statement", but rather was dipping into "cookie-jar reserves".[33] Finally, the currency options business at the NAB was not "misrepresenting the true value of the currency options portfolio", it was "smoothing".

When we fail to incorporate the ethical dimension of a dilemma into the language we use, it is easy to completely overlook the ethical dimension.

ADVANTAGEOUS COMPARISON

Unethical conduct can be seen to be quite acceptable when it is compared to more flagrant and reprehensible behaviour. In environments predicated by immoral norms and inappropriate conduct, it is easy for someone to allow their standards to slip and still feel righteous. Provided they consider their behaviour to be less egregious than others, then they can justify in their own minds that they have not compromised their morality.

Advantageous comparison allowed the currency options business at the NAB to morally justify the use of "smoothing". Income smoothing is a practice that is widely adopted in the corporate world.[34] What's more, it is a practice that in some cases is condoned and considered to be advantageous.[35] Because it is a clandestine practice, one can easily justify its use on the basis that "everyone is doing it". The issue of course is that there are no formal boundaries. It is therefore easy to fall into the trap of believing that others are engaging in the practice more flagrantly, making your conduct seem less reprehensible.

DISTORTION OF CONSEQUENCES

Distortion of consequences is a mechanism that results in the deleterious consequences associated with misconduct being minimised or negated. It has particular relevance for unethical and criminal behaviour in the corporate world because of the numerous methods used by the perpetrators of corporate crime to deny their criminality, one that is often used is to describe it as a "victimless crime".[36] Claiming that unethical conduct in the business world "does no harm" is a convenient way of distancing ourselves from the potential human costs associated with our actions. When we fail to see the human dimension of our actions, we can easily absolve ourselves of any moral responsibility associated with our roles.

Neuroscientists have shown that failing to create connections with other humans not only makes us respond in a more self-centered manner, but it also alters our neurological response. In a study employing the Prisoner's Dilemma Game, James Rilling and his colleagues matched participants with both human and computer partners.[37] When they were playing with humans, not only were participants more likely to act in a cooperative manner, but a reciprocal cooperative response from their partner activated the reward regions of the brain. However, reciprocal cooperative responses from computers did not elicit similar brain activity. Similarly, Alan Sanfey and his colleagues found that not only are people more willing to accept unfair offers when playing the Ultimatum Game with a computer, but that the brain responds differently when receiving an unfair offer from a computer as opposed to a human.[38]

It is the recurring theme from chapter three visiting us again – the importance of connecting people within organisations to the communities they serve and to a virtuous social purpose cannot be underestimated. Doing this successfully will tap into our desires for fairness, equality, reciprocity and altruism. When workers become detached from their clients and communities, it is far easier to justify immoral behaviour on the basis that it "does no harm".

Lessons for Leaders

> *I was taught that the human brain was the crowning glory of evolution so far, but I think it's a very poor scheme for survival.*[39]
>
> *Kurt Vonnegut*

Overcoming the biases associated with System 1 thinking is not a straightforward task. Research that employed a number methods, including the provision of extensive coaching, feedback and training, achieved only marginal improvements in people's ability to overcome some of the cognitive biases outlined in this chapter.[40] A more recent study that employed philosophers as participants, 94 per cent of whom held PhDs, found that they were just as susceptible to framing effects as non-philosophers.[41] There is good reason for this. As described in the introduction to this chapter, the two distinct processing mechanisms that make up our cognition have evolved over millions of years, and they have enabled humans to survive and prosper. Simply reading a textbook describing the cognitive biases associated with System 1 thinking is not going to provide a remedy for helping us overcome adaptations associated with the evolutionary process, let alone make us more aware of when we effortlessly and unconsciously engage our System 1 thinking.

Instead of posing questions for leaders in this chapter, we will review some strategies that research has shown to be effective in reducing unethical behaviour caused by our faulty cognitions. Although not foolproof, the strategies are very straightforward and can easily be implemented.

MAKING ETHICS MORE SALIENT

Making the moral dimension of a situation more salient can assist in promoting ethical conduct. Nina Mazar and her colleagues conducted a study where participants who were students were required to complete a series of simple arithmetic tasks.[42] The study employed the "matrix task" subsequently used by Francesca Gino and her colleagues in a study outlined in chapter one (see Table 1.1). The participants had four minutes to solve as many of the matrices as possible, and they were rewarded based on the number they solved correctly. To determine if the size of the monetary reward would have any effect on performance, some participants were awarded $0.50 for each correctly solved matrix, while others were rewarded $2.00. In addition, the participants were randomly placed into one of three groups.

The first group completed the task under normal test conditions. The second group of students was provided with the opportunity to cheat. Upon completing the task, they were instructed to tear out the answer sheet and simply advise the experimenter of the number of problems they successfully solved. The final group was also provided with the opportunity to cheat; however, at the top of the assessment sheet, there was a statement that read "I understand that this short survey falls under <institution's name inserted here> honour system". The students in this group were required to sign their names beneath this statement prior to commencing the task.

The results, illustrated in Figure 4.3, provided two findings. Firstly, the size of the monetary reward offered to students did not impact on their performance. Secondly, when participants were provided with the opportunity to cheat, their performance improved significantly, suggesting that they availed themselves of the opportunity to do so. However, when the participants were required to sign the reference to their institution's honour code, their performance levels returned to baseline despite the opportunity to cheat still being available to them. The honour code drew the participant's attention to their moral obligations. A more recent replication of the study showed that subconsciously priming participants by having them complete a sentence unscrambling task containing ethics-related words has the same effect.[43]

Similar to some of the studies referred to in chapter one, by making reference to the honour code Mazar and her colleagues activated the "no cheating" injunctive social norm, and this cue worked to guide behaviour. There is, however, an interesting footnote to this study that deserves mention. The universities where the study was originally conducted did not have an honour code. Furthermore, when the study was repeated at a university that had a

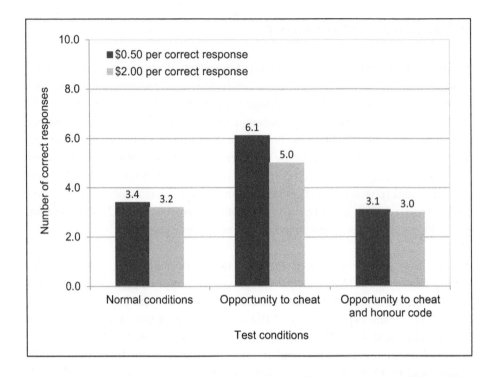

Figure 4.3   Performance in the "matrix task" in one of three scenarios: (a)
              normal test conditions, (b) opportunity for cheating, and (c)
              opportunity for cheating and requirement to sign honour code.
              In each scenario, some students were awarded $0.50 for each
              correctly solved matrix, while others were awarded $2.00

Source: Mazar, N., Amir, O., & Ariely, D. (2008). The dishonesty of honest people:
A theory of self-concept maintenance. *Journal of Marketing Research, 45*(6), 633–644.
Reprinted with permission, published by the American Marketing Association.

strict honour code, the pattern of results were almost identical. This further
reinforces one of the key lessons from chapter one – there is no substitute for
senior leaders undertaking the hard work required to bring a code of ethics to
life, and, through their actions, choices and decisions, creating an environment
that fosters behaviours that are aligned to the document. If we expect a code of
ethics to do its job by miraculously appearing like a guardian angel each time
someone is facing a dilemma, then it will inevitably fail.

TIME

There are now numerous studies that illustrate how providing a person with
more time whenever they are confronted with an ethical dilemma tends to lead

to a more virtuous decision being made. The seminal study of this nature was conducted by John Darley and Daniel Batson in the 1970s, where students from the Princeton Theological Seminary were recruited as participants and required to deliver a presentation in a separate building.[44] Some of the participants were asked to give a talk on careers for seminary students, while others were asked to give a talk on the parable of the Good Samaritan. In addition, these two groups were further divided such that some of the participants were time poor and told they were running late, while others were asked to begin making their way to the separate building despite there being ample time.

On their way, the participants encountered an accomplice of the experimenters in an alley who staged being in distress and requiring assistance. The variable that determined whether the participants stopped to render assistance was not the topic of the presentation they were about to deliver, but how much time they had. As Darley and Batson stated:

> Indeed, on several occasions, a seminary student going to give his talk on the parable of the Good Samaritan literally stepped over the victim as he hurried on his way!

More recently, a number of studies have shown that providing participants facing a dilemma with more time can increase ethical behaviour.[45] One of the explanations put forward to explain these findings is that time allows people to contemplate and engage the effortful thinking associated with System 2. Support for this proposition is provided by research which shows that when deliberating right versus right moral dilemmas, participants under time pressure provide responses suggesting the use of an "intuitive emotional" cognitive process (analogous to System 1 thinking).[46] However, when there was no time pressure, the responses to the same dilemmas differed and suggested that a "controlled cognitive" process (analogous to System 2 thinking) was engaged.

Whatever the case may be, time constraints, just like an obsessive focus on ambitious goals discussed in chapter three, can enhance pressure. The addition of pressure to factors like power and lucrative monetary rewards creates an environment fertile for unethical conduct. It is little wonder that financial markets, where all of these variables are in play, has bred its fair share of ethical scandals. Where possible, leaders should look to institute practices that encourage contemplation and extend the time taken for decisions to be made, especially those with ethical consequence. Arguably, the primary benefit associated with any ethical decision making framework is that they force people to stop, reflect, and consider the ethical consequences of their decision.

FATIGUE

Navigating right versus wrong dilemmas requires us to display self-control. As this book has demonstrated, there are a wide range of situations that can seduce us into behaving in immoral ways, and when placed in these situations, we must self-regulate. Psychologists investigating self-control have consistently found that when people are put in situations where they must show restraint and exercise self-control, it is subsequently more difficult for them to do so. This has led to the development of the "strength" or "energy" model for self-control, which proposes that self-control is a limited resource which depletes.[47] Thus, if we have been engaged in mentally demanding activities (for example, dealing with stress, being constantly vigilant, deep concentration or resisting temptations), we will find that our ability to self-regulate and exercise self-control is compromised.

This pattern of behaviour has been demonstrated in research where participants, after engaging in an activity that requires them to self-regulate, are subsequently placed in situations where they are provided with the opportunity to behave immorally. In two such studies, participants were divided into two groups.[48] Both groups were asked to write a short essay, with the first group asked not to use any words containing the letters X and Y, and the second group asked not to use any words containing the letters A and N. Given there are far more words in the English language containing the letters A and N, this latter task is mentally demanding and requires greater self-control, as participants must inhibit their natural writing tendencies. After completing this exercise, participants were provided with the opportunity to cheat in the previously explained "matrix task" employed by Nina Mazar and her colleagues. In both studies, the participants who were required to display greater self-control in the essay-writing task cheated far more in the "matrix task".

Field studies have also shown that there can be moral consequences associated with making decisions when our cognitive resources are depleted. In an ingenious study conducted by Shai Danziger and his colleagues, the rulings on parole requests made by eight Jewish–Israeli judges over a ten-month period were analysed.[49] It was found that the probability of judges providing prisoners with favourable rulings was markedly higher at the beginning of the day and just after their two scheduled food breaks. As judges sequentially presided over a series of requests, the likelihood of a favourable ruling steadily declined.[50] Meanwhile, Michael Christian and Aleksander Ellis conducted a study of 171 nurses working at a major medical centre in the US.[51] They found that nurses who were sleep deprived (defined as having slept six or fewer hours in the night prior to their shift), were shown to exhibit reduced self-control and increased workplace deviance.

What these findings demonstrate is that when our mental reserves are fatigued or depleted, we may find it difficult to engage the deep, effortful, deliberative thinking associated with System 2 that is required to navigate ethical dilemmas. It is therefore vital that we build meaningful breaks into our work schedule, not just within the working day, but also across the working week and year. These breaks should be used to rest, reflect and rejuvenate, allowing us to replenish our cognitive reserves.

BRING ETHICS INTO THE VERNACULAR

This chapter has shown the powerful role language plays in shaping how we look at and respond to a dilemma. Despite this, it would be the exception rather than the rule when deliberating a "business decision" that the ethical dimension associated with the decision is brought into the discussion. What's more, we have also seen how simply labelling a decision as purely commercial can make us totally overlook the ethics associated with it. The lesson here is very straightforward – make ethics part of the language in the workplace. More importantly, make it a practice to deliberately set some time aside to discuss the ethical dimension when you or a group are making decisions.

Ting Zhang and her colleagues conducted a study that also showed how the language used when contemplating a dilemma can lead to greater moral insight.[52] When confronted with a range of ethical dilemmas that involved competing moral virtues (the classic "right versus right" dilemmas), Zhang and her colleagues found that most people default to asking themselves "What should I do?". However, by prompting participants to approach the dilemmas asking "What could I do?", people were far more likely to display divergent thinking and consider multiple possibilities – they no longer viewed the dilemma as one that contained forced trade-offs. This change in approach cultivated greater moral insight and more creative solutions. Once again, this study illustrates the power of language – just a minor change in phrase can have a profound effect on mindset and approach.

THE "PRE-MORTEM"

In his book *Thinking Fast and Slow*, Daniel Kahneman introduces the concept of the "pre-mortem", an idea he attributes to Gary Klein. Kahneman proposes that the pre-mortem is one way of partially addressing the potential pitfalls associated with overconfidence, noting that overconfidence and optimism are features of System 1 thinking that will never be totally overcome. The process underpinning the pre-mortem is reasonably straightforward. When a group is coming close to making an important decision, people who are knowledgeable with the decision come together and imagine that they are one year into the future and the outcome is a total disaster. Each person privately brainstorms what this would look like and what has occurred over that 12-month period to drive the disaster. They then share their thoughts with the group.

There are several features of the pre-mortem that make it a powerful exercise. Firstly, by having people brainstorm scenarios privately, it attempts to overcome the likelihood of dysfunctional group dynamics railroading the discussion and failing to uncover some potential issues or events that may drive adverse outcomes. Secondly, it forces people to "consider the opposite" by imagining and documenting what failure potentially could look like.[53] In the lead-up to most decisions, a group tends to converge in its opinions and fails to consider the possibility that things may not go as planned. Finally, it is easy to introduce ethics into the process by having individuals also brainstorm what would have happened over the intervening period if one year from now the decision turned out to be a total ethical disaster.

Notes

[1]   Kahneman, D. (2011). *Thinking fast and slow*. New York, NY: Farrar, Straus and Giroux.

[2]   For an excellent historical perspective on how this theory evolved, see: Frankish, K., & Evans, J. St. B. T. (2009). The duality of mind: An historical perspective. In J. Evans & K. Frankish (Eds.), *In two minds: Dual processes and beyond* (pp. 1–29). Oxford, UK: Oxford University Press.

[3]   Kahneman, D. (2011).

[4]   Chugh, D., Bazerman, M. H., & Banaji, M. R. (2005). Bounded ethicality as a psychological barrier to recognizing conflicts of interest. In D. A. Moore, D. M. Cain, G. Loewenstein, & M. H. Bazerman (Eds.), *Conflict of interest: Challenges and solutions in business, law, medicine, and public policy* (pp. 74–95). New York, NY: Cambridge University Press.

[5]   Haidt, J. (2001). The emotional dog and its rational tail: A social intuitionist approach to moral judgment. *Psychological Review, 108*(4), 814–834.

6   Greene, J. D., Nystrom, L. E., Engell, A. D., Darley, J. M., & Cohen, J. D. (2004). The neural bases of cognitive conflict and control in moral judgment. *Neuron, 44*(2), 389–400.

7   See for example: Bazerman, M. H., & Moore, D. A. (2009). *Judgment in Managerial Decision Making* (8th ed.). Hoboken, NJ: John Wiley and Sons.

8   Lewis, C. S. (1942). *The screwtape letters.* New York, NY: HarperCollins Publishers.

9   Readers should rest assured that the parable is purely metaphorical, and that a frog will detect the danger and jump out of a vessel containing water that is slowly being brought to boil (at least according to Wikipedia): Boling frog. Retrieved December 15, 2015, from http://en.wikipedia.org/wiki/Boiling_frog

10   Gino, F., & Bazerman, M. H. (2009). When misconduct goes unnoticed: The acceptability of gradual erosion in others' ethical behavior. *Journal of Experimental Social Psychology, 45*(4), 708–719.

11   The following information is taken from: Australian Prudential Regulatory Authority. (2004, March 23). *Report into irregular currency options trading at the National Australia Bank.* Sydney, Australia: Author; PricewaterhouseCoopers. (2004, March 12). *Investigation into foreign exchange losses at the National Australia Bank.* Melbourne, Australia: Author.

12   The measure of risk most commonly used in financial markets is Value at Risk (VaR). To measure VaR, the market rates used to calculate the value of the assets in the portfolio are stressed. The resulting worst case change in the value of the portfolio given these movements in rates is the VaR.

13   Tversky, A., & Khaneman, D. (1981). The framing of decisions and the psychology of choice. *Science, 211*(4481), 453–458.

14   Kahneman, D., & Tversky, A. (1979). Prospect theory: An analysis of decision under risk. *Econometrica, 47*(2), 263–291.

15   Kern, M. C., & Chugh, D. (2009). Bounded ethicality: The perils of loss framing. *Psychological Science, 20*(3), 378–384.

16   Liberman, V., Samuels, S. M., & Ross, L. (2004). The name of the game: Predictive power of reputations versus situational labels in determining Prisoner's Dilemma Game moves. *Personality and Social Psychology Bulletin, 30*(9), 1175–1185.

17   Tenbrunsel, A. E., & Messick, D. M. (1999). Sanctioning systems, decision frames, and cooperation. *Administrative Science Quarterly, 44*(4), 684–707.

[18] Kouchaki, M., Smith-Crowe, K., Brief, A. P., & Sousa, C. (2013). Seeing green: Mere exposure to money triggers a business decision frame and unethical outcomes. *Organizational Behavior and Human Decision Processes, 121*(1), 53–61.

[19] Harris, S. B. (2010). *The moral landscape: How science can determine human values.* New York, NY: Free Press.

[20] Schrand, C. M., & Zechman, S. L. C. (2012). Executive overconfidence and the slippery slope to financial misreporting. *Journal of Accounting and Economics, 53*(1–2), 311–329.

[21] For an early review, see: Lichtenstein, S., Fischhoff, B., & Phillips, L. D. (1982). Calibration of probabilities: The state of the art to 1980. In: D. Kahneman, P. Slovic, & A. Tversky (Eds.), *Judgment under uncertainty: Heuristics and biases* (pp. 306–334). Cambridge, UK: Cambridge University Press.

[22] Barber, B. M., & Odean, T. (2000). Trading is hazardous to your wealth: The common stock investment performance of individual investors. *The Journal of Finance, 55*(2), 773–806; Barber, B. M., & Odean, T. (2013). The behaviour of individual investors. In G. M. Constantinides, M. Harris, & R. M. Stulz (Eds.), *Handbook of the economics of finance* (Vol. 2A, pp. 1533–1570). Oxford, UK: Elsevier.

[23] There is significant empirical evidence supporting this observation. As a starting point, a review of the SPIVA® Scorecards produced by S&P Dow Jones Indices don't paint a pretty picture for professional investors: S&P Dow Jones Indices. Retrieved December 15, 2015, from https://us.spindices.com/

[24] Lord, C. G., Ross, L., & Lepper, M. R. (1979). Biased assimilation and attitude polarization: The effects of prior theories on subsequently considered evidence. *Journal of Personality and Social Psychology, 37*(11), 2098–2109.

[25] Park, J., Konana, P., Gu, B., Kumar, A., & Raghunathan, R. (2010). *Confirmation bias, overconfidence, and investment performance: Evidence from stock message boards.* (Research Paper Series No. IROM-07-10). Austin, TX: McCombs Business School. Retrieved December 15, 2015, from http://ssrn.com/abstract=1639470

[26] Choi, D., & Lou, D. (2010). *A test of the self-serving attribution bias: Evidence from mutual funds.* Paper presented at the fourth Singapore International Conference on Finance. Retrieved December 15, 2015, from http://ssrn.com/abstract=1100786

[27] Langer, E. J. (1975). The illusion of control. *Journal of Personality and Social Psychology, 32*(2), 311–328.

[28] Fenton-O'Creevy, M., Nicholson, N., Soane, E., & Willman, P. (2003). Trading on illusions: Unrealistic perceptions of control and trading performance. *Journal of Occupational and Organizational Psychology, 76*(1), 53–68.

[29] Pajares, F. (2004). *Albert Bandura: Biographical sketch*. Retrieved December 15, 2015, from http://stanford.edu/dept/psychology/bandura/bandura-bio-pajares/Albert%20_Bandura%20_Biographical_Sketch.html

[30] Shu, L. L., Gino, F., & Bazerman, M. H. (2011). Dishonest deed, clear conscience: When cheating leads to moral disengagement and motivated forgetting. *Personality and Social Psychology Bulletin, 37*(3), 330–349.

[31] Moore, C., Mayer, D. M., Chiang, F. F. T., Crossley, C. D., Karlesky, M. J., & Birtch, T. A. (2014). Leaders matter morally: The role of ethical leadership in shaping employee moral cognition and misconduct. *Social Science Research Network*. Retrieved December 15, 2015, from http://ssrn.com/abstract=2574219

[32] Bandura, A. (1990). Selective activation and disengagement of moral control. *Journal of Social Issues, 46*(1), 27–46.

[33] Dells' SEC settlement: Taking away Dell's cookie-jar. (2010, July 23). *The Economist*. Retrieved December 15, 2015, from http://www.economist.com/blogs/newsbook/2010/07/dells_sec_settlement

[34] Jenkins, D. S., Kane, G. D., & Velury, U. (2006). Earnings quality decline and the effect of industry specialist auditors: An analysis of the late 1990s. *Journal of Accounting and Public Policy, 25*(1), 71–90.

[35] Tucker, J. W., & Zarowin, P. A. (2006). Does income smoothing improve earnings informativeness? *The Accounting Review, 81*(1), 251–270.

[36] Benson, M. L. (1985). Denying the guilty mind: Accounting for involvement in a white-collar crime. *Criminology, 23*(4), 583–607.

[37] Rilling, J. K., Gutman, D. A., Zeh, T. R., Pagnoni, G., Berns, G. S., & Kilts, C. D. (2002). A neural basis for social cooperation. *Neuron, 35*(2), 395–405.

[38] Sanfey, A. G., Rilling, J. K., Aronson, J. A., Nystrom, L. E., & Cohen, J. D. (2003). The neural basis of economic decision-making in the Ultimatum Game. *Science, 300*(5626), 1755–1758.

[39] Archer, J. (1987, December 27). Sayings of the year. *The Observer*, p. 6.

[40]   Fischhoff, B. (1982). Debiasing. In D. Kahneman, P. Slovic, & A. Tversky (Eds.), *Judgment under uncertainty: Heuristics and biases* (pp. 422–444). Cambridge, UK: Cambridge University Press.

[41]   Schwitzgebel, E., & Cushman, F. (2015). Philosophers' biased judgments persist despite training, expertise and reflection. *Cognition, 141*, 127–137.

[42]   Mazar, N., Amir, O., & Ariely, D. (2008). The dishonesty of honest people: A theory of self-concept maintenance. *Journal of Marketing Research, 45*(6), 633–644.

[43]   Welsh, D. T., & Ordóñez, L. D. (2014). Conscience without cognition: The effects of subconscious priming on ethical behaviour. *Academy of Management Journal, 57*(3), 723–742.

[44]   Darley, J. M., & Batson, C. D. (1973). From Jerusalem to Jericho: A study of situational and dispositional variables in helping behaviour. *Journal of Personality and Social Psychology, 27*(1), 100–108.

[45]   See for example: Gino, F., & Mogilner, C. (2014). Time, money and morality. *Psychological Science, 25*(2), 414–421; Gunia, B. C., Wang, L., Huan, L., Wang, J., & Murnighan, J. K. (2012). Contemplation and conversation: Subtle influences on moral decision making. *Academy of Management Journal, 55*(1), 13–33; Kern, M. C., & Chugh, D. (2009); Shalvi, S., Eldar, O., & Bereby-Meyer, Y. (2012). Honesty requires time (and lack of justifications). *Psychological Science, 23*(10), 1264–1270.

[46]   Suter, R. S., & Hertwig, R. (2011). Time and moral judgement. *Cognition, 119*(3), 454–458.

[47]   Baumeister, R. F., & Heatherton, T. F. (1996). Self-regulation failure: An overview. *Psychological Inquiry, 7*(1), 1–15; Baumeister, R. F., Vohs, K. D., & Tice, D. M. (2007). The strength model of self-control. *Current Directions in Psychological Science, 16*(6), 351–355; Heatherton, T. F., & Baumeister, R. F. (1996). Self-regulation failure: Past, present, and future. *Psychological Inquiry, 7*(1), 90–98.

[48]   Gino, F., Schweitzer, M. E., Mead, N. L., & Ariely, D. (2011). Unable to resist temptation: How self-control depletion promotes unethical behavior. *Organizational Behavior and Human Decision Processes, 115*(2), 191–203; Mead, N. L., Baumeister, R. F., Gino, F., Schweitzer, M. E., & Ariely, D. (2009). Too tired to tell the truth: Self-control resource depletion and dishonesty. *Journal of Experimental Social Psychology, 45*(3), 594–597.

[49]   Danziger, S., Levav, J., & Avnaim-Presso, L. (2011). Extraneous factors in judicial decisions. *Proceedings of the National Academy of Sciences of the United States of America, 108*(17), 6889–6892.

[50] It is worth noting that although the authors use "mental depletion" as an explanation for their findings, they also state that they cannot unequivocally prove that this is the case because they "do not have a direct measure of the judges' mental resources".

[51] Christain, M. S., & Ellis, A. P. J. (2011). Examining the effects of sleep deprivation on workplace deviance: A self-regulatory perspective. *Academy of Management Journal, 54*(5), 913–934.

[52] Zhang, T., Gino, F., & Margolis, J. (2014). *Does "could" lead to good? Toward a theory of moral insight.* (Working Paper No. 14-118). Boston, MA: Harvard Business School. Retrieved December 15, 2015, from http://hbswk.hbs.edu/item/does-could-lead-to-good-toward-a-theory-of-moral-insight

[53] Lord, C. G., Lepper, M. R., & Preston, E. (1984). Considering the opposite: A corrective strategy for social judgment. *Journal of Personality and Social Psychology, 47*(6), 1231–1243.

Conclusion

Leaders live in the gap between what should be and what is. That is where the work that most needs doing resides. On one side of the gap, our dreams, our aspirations our best hopes for each other and our communities call to us. The other side is the world as we know it: Beset with human frailty, strife and pent up hope. It is here amidst complex and competing forces that pull and yank on their time and beliefs that leaders do their work. It takes guts to set forth and endure life in this gap; there is no golden bullet or magic fix.[1]

Harry Barnes

So, "Why can't the banking industry solve its ethics problems?"[2] There are no straightforward answers to this question. As this book has shown, explanations for ethical failures are complex and multidimensional. Contexts punctuated by immoral norms that are endorsed by the behaviours of senior leaders, dysfunctional group dynamics, flawed incentive systems, the corrupting influence of money and power, the fear associated with loss of status, cognitive processes that default to unethical behaviour outside our conscious awareness, not to mention regulatory, operational, governance and compliance failures, topics not covered in this book. In many ways, it is actually surprising we don't see more incidents of unethical conduct. No organisation is foolproof.

Despite this, we should not throw our hands up in despair. There are steps that can be taken to build ethical cultures and inoculate organisations against the likelihood of ethical failures. This being said, there is no silver bullet, and the effort required is significant. As outlined in the introduction, the reason for this is the nature of the challenge. Building ethical cultures is adaptive work, and there is no such thing as a technical solution – no "six-point plan" or "ten habits" or "three must dos". Challenges of this type, like all adaptive work, can only be solved through thinking, practice, reflection and hard work. Ultimately, a deep understanding of what is required to promote ethical practice can only be achieved by acquiring a deep appreciation for our humanness.

As mentioned in chapter one, a good starting point for creating an ethical workplace is the articulation of a virtuous purpose that is underpinned by noble values. The challenging adaptive work involves bringing these statements of intent to life. It goes without saying that it is work well worth undertaking and investing heavily into. An ethical base must be the foundation of any organisation, and failing to build it properly means that anything that sits on top of it will be a proverbial house of cards. At their simplest, ethical failures are the result of organisations and industries failing to stay true to the values they espouse, and this breeds loss of trust. When an organisation loses the trust of the community of people it claims to serve, it is doomed to fail.

Before summarising the key lessons for leaders emanating from this book, I will explore the role of education and the chief ethics officer.

Education

> *Changing one's views of the world requires a deepened consciousness, the vulnerable contemplation of one's own thinking and value systems in order to gain clarity as to what is important, and then to take actions that align one's own deeply held intentions and desires with the greater good of humanity.*[3]
>
> *Gonzaga University, Doctoral Program in Leadership Studies*

In some quarters, the rise of unethical behaviour in the business world has been attributed to the education leaders receive in business schools. With studies showing that students taking economics majors display more positive attitudes towards greed and self-interested behaviour,[4] critics have called for a greater emphasis on ethics in the curriculum of business schools. Although there is no doubt still room for improvement, there has been a significant increase in the focus on ethics within business schools over the past decade.[5] However, I would argue that the content of these courses requires equal or even more attention. Although I am in no way an expert in pedagogy, I would like to offer a view on this topic from the perspective of a practitioner.

Traditionally, ethics courses at business schools have subscribed to the normative approach to business ethics and have had a heavy focus on moral philosophy. Specifically, provided there are appropriate rules and regulatory frameworks in place, the difference between what is "right" and "wrong" is self-evident. Therefore, teaching students how to navigate right versus wrong dilemmas was considered to be superfluous. Rather, business schools focused on grounding students in the numerous theories underpinning normative ethics such as deontology and consequentialism. The thinking went that this would provide students with the necessary tools to address the excruciating right versus right dilemmas. If ever they faced a dilemma of this nature, they would simply select the normative theory that provided the most appropriate decision-making framework given the circumstances, and voilà, the dilemma would be solved.

As we have seen, life is never this straightforward. What's more, many of the ethical failures we have witnessed in the business world over the past 15 to 20 years have involved right versus wrong dilemmas, illustrating that practitioners do not behave in the rational manner that the normative approach dictates. As outlined in the introduction, the field of behavioural business ethics emerged largely to try to address the shortcomings of the normative approach. Thankfully, the teachings from this field, many of them outlined in this book, are slowly beginning to form part of the syllabus of ethics courses at business schools, especially in North America.[6] This is a promising evolution, because at a minimum, we should be teaching business students that we are all fallible, and showing them the types of factors that can deleteriously shape our moral characters.

Even more promising is that some of these teachings are also beginning to form part of the curriculum at secondary schools. Organisations like the Heroic Imagination Project (founded by Philip Zimbardo of Stanford Prison Experiment fame) have developed programmes that teach secondary school students about group dynamics like the bystander effect and the power of social situations.[7] One of the key aims of these types of programmes is to illustrate how we all play a role in standing up to inappropriate behaviour. In many ways, it seems strange that it has taken us so long to inject some social skills training into the secondary school curriculum, given that the majority of the issues we face in life, especially ethical ones, involve some type of interpersonal process. No amount of training in calculus or grammar can prepare you for that.

Although these recent shifts are positive, my view is that there is still room for much improvement. No amount of teaching, in the traditional sense of the word, can prepare people for the challenges, discomfort, uncertainty and risk associated with facing a real-life ethical dilemma in the workplace. What's more, no amount of theoretical training can equip leaders with the moral courage required to navigate them. Leadership courses must create an environment where people feel challenged – if moral courage is what is required then leaders, as part of their training, should be put in situations where they are required to draw on it. Only then will they experience all the emotions and vulnerability associated with being in a high-pressure situation that requires them to draw on their moral reserves.

Furthermore, business schools should also aim to provide a transformational experience for their students, and have them engage in the self-reflection required to cultivate a deeper self-awareness. As discussed in chapter three, only when we do this can we begin to understand our deepest desires and what we truly care about, making us less susceptible to the trappings of success and power. Deepened self-awareness also increases our understanding of how we fit into the world, allowing us to articulate a personal vision that empowers us to make contributions that stretch far beyond ourselves. Once again, learning of the transformational kind is not easy and is personally challenging. As Gianpiero Petriglieri states, "We seldom visit the periphery of our knowledge and competence – the region where transformational learning happens – without feeling threatened, exposed, or ashamed."[8]

In short, business schools, in addition to challenging participants intellectually, must also challenge them emotionally and spiritually. Admittedly, designing courses that achieve this is no easy task, and what's more, sticking to traditional teaching techniques and curriculums is a safe option for business schools. Challenges of the intellectual kind can be mastered, and students are rarely made to feel uncomfortable in the process. In addition, it is far easier to measure progress for intellectual learning – the same can't be said when considering someone's emotional or spiritual growth.

Fortunately, there are some business schools showing leadership in this area and filling the void. Giving Voice to Values, an initiative founded by Mary Gentile, is one example.[9] Gentile admits she developed the Giving Voice to Values curriculum after a personal "crisis of faith" with traditional approaches. Among other things, the curriculum contains role plays where participants are required to act on an ethical dilemma and challenge their peers, thus creating an environment where people must draw on their moral courage. Programmes like these work to exercise our moral muscle, making it easier for us to engage it when the situation calls for it.

Hopefully it won't be long before this type of experiential learning becomes more mainstream, and replaces many of the traditional approaches to learning in our business schools.

Chief Ethics Officer

Memento mori.

Spoken by a public slave in the Roman triumph march

The role of the chief ethics officer has gained prominence over the past decade, especially in North America. This is largely in response to the regulatory burden imposed on the back of the numerous ethical scandals that have plagued the business world. In some quarters, the appointment of a chief ethics officer has been labelled as nothing more than "window dressing", and in many instances this may be the case.[10] However, although I am not suggesting that the appointment of a chief ethics officer safeguards a company against ethical lapses, I believe the role can make a significant difference if it is appropriately structured and the person in the role is given the requisite platform and mandate.

A lot has been written about the role of chief ethics officer. Much of this literature has attempted to address the following types of questions: Who should they report to? What is their scope? What is their background and qualifications?[11] There appears to be broad consensus on several of these questions. Firstly, the role of chief ethics officer must be endorsed from the highest levels (preferably the board) and be given a genuine "seat at the table". Among other things, this type of platform is symbolic. The chief ethics officer must also be independent, have no conflicts of interest and be able to freely raise matters of concern and "speak truth to power". They must have a close and supportive working relationship with the board and ultimately be responsible for carrying out their fiduciary duties. Finally, it also goes without saying that the chief ethics officer must play a central role in the development, refinement and communication of an organisation's purpose and values.

Beyond this, chief ethics officers have traditionally been placed in charge of an organisation's ethics and compliance programmes. In most cases, the focus of these programmes has been risk assessment and mitigation, the latter being achieved primarily through the use of governance and compliance frameworks, and employee training. However, I would argue (perhaps not surprisingly given the focus of this book) that the role of the chief ethics officer should be far broader than this. If the ultimate goal is to build an ethical culture, then by extension the chief ethics officer must be doing their utmost to ensure a context is being created within their organisations that promotes ethical behaviour.

From a practitioner's perspective, what does this mean? Let me begin by posing a list of questions which, although not exhaustive, will serve to illustrate the type of work a chief ethics officer should engage in to shape a system that promotes ethical conduct: Which people occupy the bases of power and are the centres of influence within the organisation? Are we comfortable that the individuals in these positions are ethical role models and the type of people we want influencing the system? Does a succession plan exist for these roles? Do you, when required, appropriately challenge, coach, counsel and influence the people in these roles? Are there leadership teams in the organisation with dysfunctional dynamics? Are the leaders of these teams aware of this and the suboptimal outcomes this is creating? Are performance and reward programmes creating an obsessive focus on goal achievement or financial reward? Are leaders displaying rent-seeking behaviour suggesting that they are more interested in serving themselves, rather than the organisation's purpose and values? Are we helping our leaders develop a deeper self-awareness and appreciation for their broader responsibilities to the communities they serve? Do we educate our leaders on their unconscious biases and their ability to act in unethical ways without realising it?

In order to shape a system that promotes ethical conduct, the chief ethics officer must have a deep understanding of adaptive change and the skills required to drive change in complex systems. Companies have traditionally filled the role with professionals from legal and compliance backgrounds. Although experience in this domain might be helpful, it is far from sufficient – the role requires someone with far broader experience. Yes, understanding how to design and monitor risk and compliance frameworks is important, but as mentioned in the introduction, character and morality cannot be regulated. The position would be better served by someone with strong commercial experience, knowledge in systems thinking, a track record of driving positive, sustainable change, and a background in psychology. Arguably, they should be more closely aligned with the human resources department, rather than the in-house audit or legal teams.

In my mind, the role of the chief ethics officer is analogous to that played by a public slave during the triumph marches held in ancient Roman times. Legend has it that after a successful military conquest, the commander was sanctified and commemorated by adorning him in regal clothing and having him participate in a public march in a horse-drawn chariot.[12] The commander was for all intents and purposes given the status of "king for a day", yet despite this, was required to conduct himself with humility and dignity. To enable this, a public slave would act as his companion, and from time to time remind the commander of his mortality by speaking the words *"momento mori"* (remember that you have to die). The chief ethics officer too must be provided with the authority to speak truth to and challenge senior leaders, keeping them grounded and aware of their responsibilities and obligations to the people, organisations and communities they serve.

Lessons for Leaders

> *... men are themselves responsible for having become careless through living carelessly ... They acquire a particular quality by constantly acting in a particular way.*
>
> *Aristotle,* Nicomachean Ethics

With the passage of time I have come to realise that my experience was in many ways a gift. It has provided me with some incredible insight and lessons into the origins of unethical conduct within orgnaisations. My hope is that through this book I have shared some of these insights and lessons with you.

The objective of the "Lessons for Leaders" sections at the conclusion of each chapter was to prompt some reflection on what is currently occurring both in your workplace and with your own personal leadership journey. If the questions that were posed made it seem like solutions to potential ethical issues are straightforward, I apologise. They are not. As I have mentioned, there is no easy fix, just thinking, practice, reflection and a lot of hard work.

Of the many lessons that my experience provided, I value three most highly. Firstly, we are all susceptible – our moral character is not fixed, it's malleable. Research shows that all of us can display moral hypocrisy, behaving in self-interested ways despite recognising that doing so is immoral.[13] This book illustrates how this tendency we all have to occasionally be dishonest and push moral boundaries can blow out and culminate into scandalous, unethical behaviour. In presentations I have delivered on this topic, I often ask the audience to raise their hands if they think they are capable of being involved in an ethical failure. Typically, far less than 50 per cent of the audience raise their hand, a response that is not surprising given that we are overconfident and notoriously poor predictors of our future behaviour. My advice to the people who don't raise their hands is not to be so sure. When given the choice between being humble and being humiliated, choose the former.

Secondly, although when I talk to some leaders I reluctantly accept their claims that they are above improper behaviour, one thing I am not prepared to accept is that they are incapable of overseeing an ethical failure. The senior leaders of all organisations play a central role in shaping the context that incubates ethical failures. What's more, as leaders, it doesn't matter whether you were personally involved in improper conduct, or for that matter whether you knew that your people were engaging in it. Rather, the question is, should you have known? Did you miss or overlook the signals that could have alerted you to unethical conduct, and thus fail to take necessary corrective action?

In some instances, those signals can be very subtle, and only with the benefit of hindsight do we recognise that these subtle signals were actually blaring alarms. However, what is more often the case is that leaders display "motivated blindness" – they fail to recognise the signals because it is convenient for them to do so. This book has illustrated the multiple ways in which we can engage in motivated blindness: in-group favouritisim, not wanting to challenge our peers or leaders as a result of dysfunctional group dynamics, a myopic focus on goals, the lure of rewards provided by flawed incentive frameworks, our desire to protect our status and power, framing something as a "business decision", and the list goes on. For leaders, it is not just about ensuring one's own conduct is above board, but in the words of Max Bazerman, we must also learn how to become "first class noticers".[14]

Finally, although it sounds clichéd, my experience illustrated to me the power of choice. Very few people will face a choice in their careers as dramatic as the one I faced, the proverbial fork in the road. What's more, I have come to recognise that it is not these types of dramatic "defining moment" choices that shape the ethical fabric of an organisation. When circumstances have decayed to the point where a whistleblower is required, then several wrong turns were taken some time back and never redressed. Rather, it is the smaller choices that leaders make that send subtle signals, and over time they culminate and slowly but surely establish a tone of ethical conduct within an organisation. The cumulative impact of these smaller choices is to strengthen the moral resiliency of the organisation and the ethical resolve of the leader, making it progressively easier for them to choose the ethical route. As Erich Fromm so eloquently puts it in his book *The Heart of Man*:[15]

> *Each step in life which increases my self-confidence, my integrity, my courage, my conviction also increases my capacity to choose the desirable alternative, until eventually it becomes more difficult to choose the undesirable rather than the desirable action. On the*

other hand, each act of surrender and cowardice weakens me, opens the path for more acts of surrender, and eventually freedom is lost. Between the extreme when I can no longer do a wrong act, and the other extreme when I have lost my freedom to right action, there are innumerable degrees of freedom of choice. In the practice of life the degree of freedom to choose is different at any given moment. If the degree of freedom to choose the good is great, it needs less effort to choose the good. If it is small, it takes great effort, help from others, and favourable circumstances.

May your values be virtuous, and may your choices be aligned to your values.

Notes

[1]   Intrator, S. M., & Scribner, M. (2007). *Leading from within: Poetry that sustains the courage to lead.* San Francisco, CA: Jossey-Bass.

[2]   Irwin, N. (2014, July 29). Why can't the banking industry solve its ethics problems? *The New York Times.* Retrieved December 15, 2015, from http://www.nytimes.com/2014/07/30/upshot/why-cant-the-banking-industry-solve-its-ethics-problems.html

[3]   Gonzaga University. (2004). *Gonzaga University's Doctoral Program in Leadership Studies: A focus on the personal dimension of leadership.* Paper presented at the International Leadership Association Conference.

[4]   Wang, L., Malhotra, D., & Murnighan, J. K. (2011). Economics education and greed. *Academy of Management Learning and Education, 10*(4), 643–660.

[5]   Wright, N. S., Bennett, H. (2011). Business ethics, CSR, sustainability and the MBA. *Journal of Management and Organization, 17*(5), 641–655.

[6]   Knight, R. (2013, June 16). A business school tackles ethics. *Financial Times.* Retrieved December 15, 2015, from http://www.ft.com/intl/cms/s/0/c6a81cdc-66e8-11e2-a805-00144feab49a.html#axzz3JIK3zHlR

[7]   Heroic Imagination Project (HIP). Retrieved December 15, 2015, from http://heroicimagination.org/

[8]   Petriglieri, G. (2014, November 6). Learning is the most celebrated neglected activity in the workplace. *Harvard Business Review.* Retrieved December 15, 2015, from https://hbr.org/2014/11/learning-is-the-most-celebrated-neglected-activity-in-the-workplace

⁹   Gentile, M. C. (2012). Values-driven leadership development: Where we have been and where
    we could go. *Organization Management Journal, 9*(3), 188–196.

¹⁰ Clark, H. (2006, October 23). Chief Ethics Officers: Who needs them? *Forbes.* Retrieved
    December 15, 2015, from http://www.forbes.com/2006/10/23/leadership-ethics-hp-lead-govern-
    cx_hc_1023ethics.html

¹¹ See for example: Ethics Resource Centre. (2007, September). *Leading corporate integrity: Defining
    the role of the Chief Ethics and Compliance Officer (CECO).* Retrieved December 15, 2015, from
    http://www.corporatecompliance.org/Resources/View/ArticleId/750/Defining-the-Role-of-the-
    Chief-Ethics-Compliance-Officer-CECO.aspx

¹² Roman triumph. Retrieved December 15, 2015, from https://en.wikipedia.org/wiki/Roman_
    triumph

¹³ Batson, C. D., Kobrynowicz, D., Dinnerstein, J. L., Kampf, H. C., Wilson, A. D. (1997). In a very
    different voice: Unmasking moral hypocrisy. *Journal of Personality and Social Psychology, 72*(6),
    1335–1348.

¹⁴ Bazerman, M. H. (2014). *The power of noticing: What the best leaders see.* New York, NY: Simon
    and Schuster.

    Bazerman credits the American writer Saul Bellow with coining the phrase "first class noticer",
    a quality he attributed to a character in his novella *The Actual.*

¹⁵ Fromm, E. (1964). *The heart of man: It's genius for good and evil.* New York, NY: Harper & Row.

Index

active fund managers, self-serving
    bias 140
advantageous comparison 143
Aggarwal, Pankaj 46
Allport, Floyd 55
altruism 81, 84, 86, 100, 144
ambitious goals, focus
    (obsessiveness) 88–9, 90–1
amygdala, activation 58, 84
Andersen, Hans Christian 55
anonymity, deindividuation 62
approach/inhibition theory
    (power) 106
Arbitrage (film) 114
Ariely, Dan 98, 100
Aristotle 28, 71, 163
Asch, Solomon 56–7; cards, usage
    (example) 57; participants,
    accomplice role 57–8; trials 57
Asian disease problem 132–3;
    framing 135; loss aversion
    133–4
attention, focus/blindness 88–9
Australia *Four Corners* program 36
Australian Wheat Board (AWB), oil-
    for-wheat scandal 35
authority figures, obedience
    (experiment) 47–54

bad apples (rogues) 7–8, 25, 36
Badaracco, Joseph 30, 102–3
Bandura, Albert 28–30, 141–2
bank employees, dishonesty norm
    compliance 15

banking industry, ethics problems 1
Barclays Bank, role 33
Barnes, Harry 157
Bathsheba Syndrome 103
Batson, Daniel 147
Bazerman, Max 129, 164
Beaman, Arthur 117
behavioural business ethics 3–4,
    79, 159
Bendahan, Samuel 103
Berkman, Elliot 84
Berns, Gregory 58
better than average effect 110
biased memory, display 110
biases 127–41; overcoming 144–50
Biggerstaff, Lee 31–2
blindness, experiment 88–9
blood donors, monetary payment 100
Bobo dolls: aggressive behaviour 30;
    experiments 29
Boettger, Richard 89
bonuses, types 90
bounded ethicality 127–8
brain activity: abstract reasoning 128;
    amygdala activity, increase 58, 84;
    preference and pleasure 95;
    physical pain 70; reward
    region activity, increase
    84–5, 111, 143–4; self-referential
    thought 117
British Broadcasting Corporation
    (BBC) prison study 22
Bromiley, Philip 91
Brosnan, Sarah 86

Buffett, Warren 88
business schools: ethics courses 158;
        transformation experiences 160
bystanders 54–6

Cadsby, Charles 89–90
Cain, Daylian 96
candle problem 99
Carney, Mark 101
Chabris, Christopher 88
Chen, Serena 110
chief ethics officer, role 161–3
Choi, Darwin 140
choice-dilemmas 60
Christian, Michael 148
Chugh, Dolly 134
Cialdini, Robert 8–10
code of ethics: institutionalise 5;
        presence 37
coercion, presence 53
cognitive dissonance 18; confirmation
        bias 139; conformity 57–8
Cohen, Leonard 102
commons dilemma 105
Community Game 135; trials,
        cooperative responses
        (percentage) 136; usage 137
confirmation bias 139
conflict of interest 96–8
conformity: Asch paradigm 56–8;
        explanations 58
conscious awareness, absence 127–8
consequences, distortion 143–4
context, power 7
control, illusion 140
cooperation: biological predisposition
        84–6; evolutionary biology 85–
        6; Prisoner's Dilemma Game
        82–5, 135–6; Ultimatum Game
        81–2, 85; Wall Street Game,
        Community Game 135–7
Coulson, Andy 35

d'Adda, Giovanna 31
Darley, John 55, 147
death, fear creation 113
decision making, biases 127–8
defining moments 30–1, 64, 164
deindividuation 61; theory,
        expansion 61–2
de Quervain, Dominique 85
descriptive norms, injunctive norms
        8–13; alignment 37; application
        19–20; deindividuation 61;
        distinction 9; salience 145–6;
        unethical descriptive norms,
        impact 9–13
de Waal, Frans 86
disidentification, process (usage) 117
distortion of consequences 143
downward comparisons 110
dual process theory, mind 127–8
Dunning-Kruger effect 111

education 158–60
ego defensiveness 110
Eisenberger, Naomi 70
electric chair, usage 48, 50, 59
Ellis, Aleksander 148
emergency, silence 55
ethical behaviour, injunctive
        norm 13
ethical champions, reward/
        promotion 38
ethical failures: Australian Wheat
        Board (AWB), oil-for-wheat
        scandal 35; Ford Pinto 53–4,
        138; global financial crisis 34;
        LIBOR rate-fixing 20, 33, 130,
        142; NAB currency options
        2–3, 18–20, 25, 28, 32–3, 46,
        53, 56, 59, 61, 68, 89–90, 128,
        130–2, 135, 143, 161; phone
        hacking scandal (UK) 34–5;
        professional cycling 20–1, 36

ethical followership 63–70
ethical leaders, moral managers 31
euphemistic labelling 142–3
evolution, principles 86
evolutionary biology 85–8
experimental economics 81–4
external validity 3–4

fairness 81, 84; biological
      predisposition 84
Fast, Nathanael 110
fatigue 148–9
fear 109–10; creation 113
Fenton-O'Creevy, Mark 140
Festinger, Leon 61
financial crisis, aftermath
      33–4
financial incentives, usage and
      impact 91–102; neuroscience
      94–5; performance and
      reward frameworks 28, 87,
      99; performance and reward
      relationship 99; social versus
      monetary 100; stifling
      creativity 99
financial markets: success 141;
      trading environment
      140–1
followership 63–6
Ford Motor Company: cost/
      benefit analysis 54; foreign
      competition 53; Pinto,
      design flaws (awareness)
      53–4; safer design, decision
      (avoidance) 138
Forsyth, Donelson 45
Foucault, Michel 80
framing 132–3, 135–42
French, John 26
Fromm, Erich 164
functional fixedness 99
fundamental attribution error 51

FX trading scandal 2–3, 18–20,
      25, 28, 46, 128; advantageous
      comparison 143; Corporate
      and Institutional Bank (CIB)
      culture 33; currency options
      portfolio Value at Risk 132;
      disapproval, silence 56;
      informal mechanisms 32–3;
      injunctive norms 20; limits,
      breaches 32; performance
      monitoring 90; portfolio value,
      overstatement amount 131;
      profit-driven morality, culture
      89; profit/loss, misstatement
      19; risk appetite 61; risk
      profile, loss aversion 135;
      slippery slope 130–1; social
      norms 18–20; team ethos,
      embracing 53

Galinsky, Adam 105–7
Gentile, Mary 160
Georgesen, John 112
Gino, Francesca 13, 92, 118, 129,
      145
Giving Voice to Values 160
global financial crisis 34
Glucksberg, Sam 99
Gneezy, Uri 100
goals: ambitious goals, focus
      (obsessiveness) 88; goal
      structure 88–9; high-
      performance benchmarks,
      imposition 89; power and goal-
      directed actions 107–9
Good Samaritan parable 147
Grant, Adam 100
Greenberg, Jeff 113
Greene, Joshua 128
group polarisation 60–3;
      emergence 60
Grover, Steven 89

Gruenfeld, Deborah 109
Guinote, Ana 108

Haidt, Jonathan 128
Hamilton, Alexander 116
Hamilton, Tyler 20
Harris, Jared 91
Harris, Monica 112
Harvey, Ann 95, 96
Haslam, Alexander 21, 22
Haun, Daniel 58
Heffernan, Margaret 68, 72, 91
Heifetz, Ronald 4
Henrich, Joseph 82
Herbert, George 132
Heroic Imagination Project 159
Heyman, James 100
Hobbes, Thomas 80
homo economicus 2, 80
Hui, Chun 89
human nature, self-interested view 80–1

Iacocca, Lee 53–4
inclusionary status, improvement 71
income statement, manipulation 143,
        91, 31–2
informal mechanisms: messages 28;
        usage 32–6
in-group: favouritism 164; social norms
        13–15
injunctive norms, descriptive norms
        8–13; alignment 37; application
        19–20; deindividuation 61;
        distinction 9; salience 145–6;
        unethical descriptive norms,
        impact 9–13
innocent bystanders 54–6
Irwin, Neil 1

Jefferson, Thomas 80
Jensen, Michael 90
Johannesson, Magnus 100

Kahneman, Daniel 127, 132, 133, 149
Kant, Immanuel 79
Kern, Mary 134
Kidder, Rushworth 63
Kierkegaard, Soren 113
King David, story 102–3
Kipnis, David 103
Kissinger, Henry 27
Klein, Gary 149
Kouchaki, Maryam 137

LaFrance, Marianne 65, 66
Langer, Ellen 140
Latane, Bibb 55
leaders: challenge, difficulty 65;
        dominant behaviour 52;
        lessons for 36, 70, 115, 144,
        163; shaping, context 25–36;
        shaping, followers (impact) 66
leadership: courses, usage 159–60;
        position, instability 109–10,
        112; role 25–36
Leveson Inquiry 34–5
Lewis, C. S. 70, 128
Lewis, Michael 19
Liberman, Varda 135, 142
LIBOR rate-fixing scandal 20, 33,
        130, 142
Lieberman, Matthew 87
linear-based bonus 90
Linksy, Marty 4
Longenecker, Clinton 103
Longstaff, Simon 37
Lord, Charles 139
loss aversion 133–5
losses, smoothing/hiding 131, 142
Lou, Dong 140
Ludwig, Dean 103

MacNeil, Mark 16–18, 58
majority influence 56–9, 73; pluralistic
        ignorance, contrast 56–7

matrix task 145; explanation 148;
performance 146
Matz, David 58
Mayar, David 69–70
Mazar, Nina 46, 145, 148
Mellstrom, Carl 100
Messick, David 137
Machiavelli, Niccolo 80
Milgram, Stanley 46–9; electric
chair, usage 48, 50, 59;
obedience experiments,
findings (implications) 51–3,
59; obedience experiments
variations 52, 54
Mill, John Stuart 54
Miller, Robert 114
Milton, John 79
mind, dual process
theory 127
mindfulness meditation 117
Mishina, Yuri 91
missionary-cannibal
dilemma 45
mnemic neglect 110
Mogilner, Cassie 118
monetary rewards usage and
impact 91–101; neuroscience
94–5; performance and
reward frameworks 28, 87,
99; performance and reward
relationship 99; social versus
monetary 100; stifling
creativity 99
Moore, Celia 111, 142
moral courage, challenging leaders
65; feature 63
moral disengagement 141–4
moral managers 31
mortality salience, terror
management theory 114
motivated forgetting 142
Murdoch, Rupert 35

narcissist, emergence 111
National Australia Bank (NAB), FX
trading scandal 2–3, 18–20,
25, 28, 46, 128; advantageous
comparison 143; Corporate
and Institutional Bank (CIB)
culture 33; currency options
portfolio Value at Risk 132;
disapproval, silence 56;
informal mechanisms
32–3; limits, breaches 32;
performance monitoring 90;
portfolio value, overstatement
amount 131; profit-driven
morality, culture 89; profit/loss,
misstatement 19; risk appetite
61; risk profile, loss aversion
135; slippery slope 130–1; team
ethos, embracing 53
natural selection 86
neuroscience 84–5; distortion of
consequences, neuroscience
143–4; group belonging,
neuroscience 70; majority
influence, neuroscience
58; monetary rewards,
neuroscience 94–5
News International 34–5
Nietzsche, Friedrich 45
normative approach 2–3, 38, 79,
158–9
Nowak, Martin 85–6

obedience: Milgram obedience
experiments 47–54,
58–9; Milgram obedience
experiments, findings
(implications) 53
oil-for-wheat scandal 35
optimal group dynamics, creation
71–2
options, backdating (practice) 31–2

organisation: code of ethics, presence
     37; defining moments 30–1;
     purpose and values 37, 64,
     99–101, 108–9, 116, 138, 144,
     158, 162
out-group, member (impact) 14
Overbeck, Jennifer 108
overconfidence 138–41; bias 140

Palmer, Parker 25
Park, Bernadette 108
Park JaeHong 139
performance 88–91; goals 89, 91;
     performance and reward
     frameworks 28, 87, 99;
     performance and reward
     relationship 99; targets, focus
     (obsession) 89
Perry, Gina 49–50, 53
personal values, understanding
     116–18
Pfeffer, Jeffrey 7
phone hacking scandal (UK) 34–5
Pierce, Lamar 16, 17, 92
Pink, Daniel 98
Pinto, design flaws/rear collisions
     53–4
pluralistic ignorance 55; explanations
     55–6; majority influence,
     contrast 56–7
Pound, Dick 36
power 102–9; approach/inhibition
     theory 106; bases of 26–7;
     corrupting influence 103–4;
     divergent effects 105–7; goals,
     moderating effect 107–10;
     obedience, group dynamics
     47–54; shaping context 25–36;
     speaking truth to 65–6, 161
pre-mortem 149–50
PricewaterhouseCoopers
     investigation 19–20, 32, 131–2

Prisoner's Dilemma Game 82–4;
     cooperative responses,
     reciprocation (neurological
     basis) 84–5; Wall Street Game,
     Community Game 135–7
prospect theory 134
public goods dilemma 105
Pyszczynski, Tom 113

Raven, Bertram 26
Reicher, Stephen 21, 22
rent seeking behaviour 101
responsibility: diffusion 55, 142;
     displacement 142
reward 91–101; monetary
     rewards, neuroscience 94–5;
     performance and reward
     frameworks 28, 87, 99;
     performance and reward
     relationship 99; social versus
     monetary 100; stifling
     creativity 99
Rilling, James 84, 95, 143
Rinpoche, Sogyal 109, 113
risky-shift phenomenon 60
Ross, Lee 51
Royal Commission, findings (oil-for-
     wheat scandal) 35
Rubinstein, Ariel 823
Rustichini, Aldo 100

Salancik, Gerald 7
Schrand, Catherine 138
Schweitzer, Maurice 90
self-awareness: cultivation 116, 160;
     development 115, 117
self-esteem: central role 110–12;
     enhancement/protection
     111; necessity, reason 113;
     protection 112; threat 111–12
self-interest axiom 80–1, 86, 91–2
self-regulation, ability 141

self-serving bias 110, 140
Shaw, Marjorie 45–6
Sherif, Muzafer 16–18, 58
Shu, Lisa 141
Simon, George 117
Simons, Daniel 88
slippery slope 128–32; explanation
        131–2
Smith, Adam 80–1
Snyder, Jason 16, 17
social dilemma games 81–2
social identity theory 13
social learning theory 28, 141
social norms 8–21; extreme norms
        16–17; group identity 13–15;
        injunctive/descriptive 8–13, 19–
        20, 37, 61, 145–6; transmission,
        generational change 16
Socrates 115
Solomon, Sheldon 113
Solzhenitsyn, Aleksandr 1
spiritual practice 117
Stanford Prison Experiment
        (SPE) 8, 21–5; criticisms 22;
        lessons 24–5; superintendent,
        role 26
status: hierarchy 28, 47, 53, 102, 109;
        protection 109–12
Staw, Barry 89
stock options, backdating 31–2
Stoner, James 60
strategic construal 111
Sunstein, Cass 60
Suu Kyi, Aung San 7

Tabibnia, Golnaz 85
Tajfel, Henri 13
target-based bonus 90
Tenbrunsel, Ann 27–8, 137
terror management theory (TMT)
        112–18

Tetlock, Philip 141
Thau, Stefan 70
time, provision 146–7
Tost, Leigh 52, 72
transformational learning 160
transparency 96–101
Tricomi, Elizabeth 85
Trost, Melanie 8
Turner, John 13
Tversky, Amos 132, 133
Twain, Mark 56

Ultimatum Game 82–4; neuroscience
        85, 144
United Nations Oil-for-Food
        Program, establishment 35
utility theory 134

values-based leaders 115
VaR position, limits (breach) 19
Veehuizen, Peter 116
Verbruggen, Hein 36
vernacular, ethics (usage) 149
Vohs, Kathleen 98
voicing disapproval 64–6
Vonnegut, Kurt 144

Wall Street Game 135, 136;
        trials, cooperative responses
        (percentage) 136; usage 137
Wargo, Donald 39
whistleblowing 66–70
Wood, Wendy 58
Woodzicka, Julie 65, 66

Zechman, Sarah 138
Zhang, Ting 149
Zimbardo, Philip 21–3, 25–6, 49,
        61, 159; heroism, perspective
        69; inhibited behaviour,
        expression 62